in **DETAIL** Exhibitions and Displays

in **DETAIL**

Exhibitions and Displays

Museum design concepts
Brand presentation
Trade show design

Christian Schittich (Ed.)

Edition DETAIL – Institut für internationale
Architektur-Dokumentation GmbH & Co. KG
München

Birkhäuser
Basel · Boston · Berlin

Editor: Christian Schittich
Project management: Steffi Lenzen
Editorial services and copy editing: Sandra Leitte, Cosima Strobl
Editorial services: Carola Jacob-Ritz, Michaela Linder,
Daniela Steffgen, Isabel Tirpitz, Melanie Weber

Translation German/English: Mark Kammerbauer

Drawings: Melanie Denys, Ralph Donhauser,
Martin Hemmel, Caroline Hörger, Nicola Kollmann,
Simon Kramer, Elisabeth Krammer, Dejanira Ornelas

DTP: Roswitha Siegler, Simone Soesters

A specialist publication from Redaktion DETAIL
This book is a cooperation between
DETAIL – Review of Architecture and
Birkhäuser – Verlag AG

Library of Congress Control Number: 2007927593

Bibliographic information published by the German National Library
The German National Library lists this publication in the Deutsche
Nationalbibliografie; detailed bibliographic data is available on the Internet at
<http://dnb.d-nb.de>.

This book is also available in a German language edition
(ISBN: 978-3-7643-9954-2).

Printed on acid-free paper produced from chlorine-free pulp (TCF ∞)

Printed in Germany
Reproduction:
Martin Härtl OHG, München
Printing and binding:
Kösel GmbH & Co. KG, Altusried-Krugzell

ISBN: 978-3-7643-9955-9

9 8 7 6 5 4 3 2 1

Contents

Designing exhibitions and presentations
Christian Schittich 8

Interaction of building and presentation – current museum concepts
Christian Schittich 10

To exhibit – From the spoon to the state
Ruedi Baur 12

Phaeno Science Center in Wolfsburg
Zaha Hadid Architects, London;
Mayer Bährle Freie Architekten, Lörrach 22

New Museum in New York
SANAA / Kazuyo Sejima + Ryue Nishizawa, Tokyo 28

Literature Museum in Marbach
David Chipperfield Architects, London/Berlin 32

Museum of Celtic and Roman History in Manching
Fischer Architekten, Munich 36

BMW Museum in Munich
ATELIER BRÜCKNER, Stuttgart 42

Mercedes-Benz Museum in Stuttgart
UNStudio, Amsterdam 52

Show and let show
HG Merz, Patrick Wais 60

"The Rommel Myth" exhibition in Stuttgart
Hans Dieter Schaal, Attenweiler 70

"That's Opera" traveling exhibition
ATELIER BRÜCKNER, Stuttgart 72

"Inventioneering Architecture" traveling exhibition
Instant Architecture, Zurich 78

Museum pavilion in Pouilly-en-Auxois
Shigeru Ban Architects, Tokyo / Paris;
Jean de Gastines, Paris 81

Exhibition pavilion for Artek in Milan
Shigeru Ban Architects, Tokyo / Paris 84

Built Identity
Architecture – Design – Communication
Jons Messedat 86

Audi Center in Munich
Allmann Sattler Wappner, Munich 96

adidas Brand Center in Herzogenaurach
querkraft Architekten, Vienna 100

Baufritz exhibition building in Erkheim
a.ml und partner, Nuremberg 104

Proper light for presentations
Thomas Schielke 108

"Freudenhaus" optician store in Munich
AIGNER ARCHITECTURE, Munich 112

Whiteleys Shopping Center in London
Lifschutz Davidson Sandilands, London 115

MPREIS Supermarket in Innsbruck
Rainer Köberl, Innsbruck 118

Edeka Supermarket in Ingolstadt
ATP Architekten und Ingenieure, Munich 122

Noise barrier with integrated car showroom near Utrecht
ONL [Oosterhuis_Lénárd], Rotterdam 126

Exhibition hall in Paris
Anne Lacaton & Jean Philippe Vassal, Paris 130

New Trade Fair in Stuttgart
Wulf & Partner, Stuttgart 134

Sustainably designing temporary architecture for brands
Susanne Schmidhuber 140

Stylepark Lounge in Berlin
J. MAYER H., Berlin 150

Exhibition stand "Garment Garden" in Frankfurt am Main
J. MAYER H., Berlin 152

Exhibition design system or custom design
Günther Röckl 154

Eternit exhibition stands in Stuttgart and Munich
Astrid Bornheim Architektur, Berlin 156

E.ON exhibition stand in Essen
avcommunication, Ludwigsburg/Munich 162

Serafini exhibition stand in Cologne
atelier 522, Markdorf 166

Architects – Project details 168

Authors 175

Illustration credits 176

Designing exhibitions and presentations

Christian Schittich

Designing exhibitions and presentations is as fascinating as it represents the current hot topic for architects, interior architects, and designers. The exhibiting of authentic objects as means of feedback with the physical world or as conveyor of interrelations of cause and effect receives special significance, especially in a world becoming more and more complex and full of digital stimuli and manipulated images. This is, for one, valid for the cultural sector, i.e. the presentation of works of art or signs of the times, but for the commercial sector as well. At the same time, within the perpetual competition with the leisure industry, the requirements that exhibitions have to meet are increasing in order to seduce the audience or offer a special experience. Architecture marks the beginning of this process more than once: By their spectacular visual appearance alone, museums become more and more expressive sculptures intended to attract streams of tourists. Simultaneously, the industry attempts to convey corporate identity and brand values through strikingly designed brand stores or trade show installations, and to communicate a corresponding life style as well.

Designing exhibitions comprises the spatial-visual implementation of a concept developed by a designer in close collaboration with curators and scientists or marketing experts. Communication with the observer and/or transmission of messages is a central goal. Architecture, regardless if exclusively designed for this purpose or already existant, plays a decisive role in this context. It sets the stage; ideally, it corresponds to the content of the presentation. Spatial compositions and proportions, illumination and visual relations can support the choreography of an exhibition and sometimes provide special opportunities. And not least the material selection and the surfaces created receive special significance.
Each exhibition places the objects on display in a new context and thus reinterprets them. The mode of presentation significantly influences its message, whether the object is a painting, an ethnological or natural historic artifact, or merchandise for sale. A carved wooden mask from Africa can be displayed as a work of art and thus an object of great cultural significance, or as a marvelous ritual object of an alien civilization. The type of dramatization, the selected colors and materials, the lighting design, explanatory graphics, as well as guidance systems, but most of all the individual compilation of exhibits greatly influence how visitors comprehend an exhibition. A conceptual central theme is of particular importance in this situation: It can be based on chronology or topic, or be constructed as narrative – an increasingly common strategy in recent time. The exhibited objects are thus contextualized or grouped according to their topic in order for them to tell a story and create suspense, similar to a good story, capturing the audience. Which path may be the better depends on the particular situation, the subject, but also the purpose and function of an exhibition. An art show featuring sculptures and paintings requires a different concept than the history of a region or the presentation of exotic butterflies, an exhibition on the opera calls for a different concept than a brand museum for the automotive industry.

Electronic media become increasingly significant. Even today, there is hardly any exhibition without audio guides or video projections. For designers and curators, the task arises to adequately integrate these media and prevent digital images from becoming autoreferential. Or, as a critic once stated, to prevent that visiting museums becomes nothing other than "public television".

As stated initially, the subject of exhibiting and presenting is as thrilling as it is diverse. In this volume, a broad range of examples, from museum to temporary exhibition, from store design to supermarket, from temporary exhibition stand to comprehensive exhibition hall, is collected and documented in detail. As far as possible, the involved creators introduce and explain their individual concept and the process of its implementation in their own words.

Interaction of building and presentation – current museum concepts

Christian Schittich

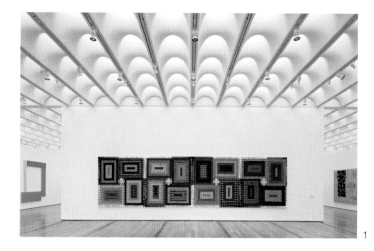

1

Who can forget the good, old-fashioned museums? On the outside mostly massive, classicist buildings with a majestic visual appearance, they often overwhelm the visitor on the inside by the sheer mass of exhibits, presented in mostly stuffy rooms and endless rows of glazed showcases. However, exhibition concepts such as these, originating in the 19th century and up to a few decades ago present in almost every European metropolis, now more or less belong to the past. Regardless whether works of art or historic technology or collections of natural history or ethnology are on display: The museum as an institution has since developed from an exalted temple of education into a glittering event environment, "wheeling and dealing" for the attention of a progressingly saturated audience. Exterior appearances have become obvious eye-catchers. The more expressive the shape, so it seems, the better the capacity for self-promotion.

Frank O. Gehry's Guggenheim Museum in Bilbao can still be considered as prototype of this kind of gesture, serving as catalyst for an entire region with its remarkable appearance. At the same time, it ignites the discussion on whether museum architecture may be permitted to take on the leading role in this way instead of serving as an unobtrusive container of special exhibits. The small literature museum in Marbach by David Chipperfield (page 32–35) impressively demonstrates that an alternative is, in fact, possible. With restrained appearance and avoiding flashy gestures, it is integrated into a landscape of hills and abstains from superfluous gimmicks. Its minimalist expression and the limited as well as exquisite material selection transform this building into a true treasure chest for the delicate exhibited manuscripts.

Peter Zumthor's Kolumba Museum in Cologne, similar to the literature museum in Marbach, is characterized by its calm nature as well as meticulously crafted details and exquisite finishes. Its striking impression is result of an appealing succession of spaces with varying proportions and lighting situations as well as dramatized views to the exterior through glazed facades from floor to ceiling. According to his own words, Zumthor intended "the opposite of the Bilbao effect", i.e. a building that was not "part of a marketing strategy", but instead the adequate enclosure for a great art collection. Thus, he designed an edifice that does not take center stage, but instead leaves space for the exhibits and still provides a special spatial and sensual experience.

In his many museum buildings, Renzo Piano emphasizes that requirements of artworks are in his view more important than possible architectural escapades. The decisive characteristic in many of his exhibition buildings is a sophisticated lighting concept both in terms of technology and design integrated into the roof structure. In order to prevent glare, he designs ingenious directional systems for natural lighting – suspended concrete louvers for the Menil Collection (1987) in Houston, Texas, or a device comprised of angled glass panels in the Fondation Beyeler (1997) in Basle. For the High Museum of Art in Atlanta, in collaboration with engineers from Arup, he designed a system of nearly 1,000 light scoops consisting of aluminum sheet metal and oriented to the north. He thus not only achieves continuous, glare-free illumination, but also a pleasantly structured ceiling within an otherwise clear interior design characterized by restraint – the design is derived from function and construction.

Jean Nouvel follows a different path in design. With the Museé du Quai Branly in Paris, he has without a doubt created one of the most spectacular museums of recent times, equally fascinating to visitors as provoking discussion among them. The grand gesture takes center stage here, especially

2

since this "Grand Projet" of former President Jacques Chirac reinterprets France's colonial heritage and dramatizes it in order to pay homage to the descendants of colonized peoples living in France today and thus integrates them into society. In contrast to the two institutes that preceded it, the collections of which have been included here are no longer presented as exotic, marvelous remnants of "primitive" peoples, but as artifacts from cultures that are equal to those of the West.

Jean Nouvel designed a heterogeneous, strikingly structured building accentuated with powerful colors, attracting attention, and possessing branding capacity. Yet at the same time it expresses its content in its exterior appearance. The grandly designed garden featuring vegetation from regions across the globe, representing the origins of the exhibits, contributes to the event factor of the institution. Upon entering, visitors ascend along a winding, 180 m long ramp onto the upper level. From here, they can freely choose a path through the four areas representing Africa, Asia, Oceania, and America. The entire 5,000 m² area of the permanent exhibition is located within a single large hall with integrated galleries and annexed niches that are reflected in the facade design as cube-shaped extrusions. A major factor of the dramatization is directed illumination. Within the space, appearing mystical and almost completely dark, individual objects are dramatized via spotlights and in particular cases staged as works of art. This kind of presentation of course is opposed to quantity: Viewers are startled that relatively few objects are on display in such a large building. In fact, only one percent of the collection's 300,000 items is on display. With this gesture, the Museé du Quai Branly becomes typical for numerous contemporary exhibition concepts. Didactics are no longer in the focus of interest. Instead, visual experience is emphasized. As result, information partially suffers under the leading role of dramatization.

The Phaeno in Wolfsburg (page 22–27) represents an interactive museum in which the visitor is not only recipient but also actively intervenes into the exhibition, i.e. becomes an actor. This so-called Science Museum intends to enable visitors to experience phenomena of natural science, most of all of physics, with all senses of perception and thus playfully to demonstrate these phenomena in an illustrative way. Seemingly vanishing into all directions, the powerful exposed concrete architecture designed by Iraqi-British architect Zaha Hadid offers the perfect setting for this special exhibition concept. Within the interior, structured by supports and organ-

ized on a polygonal floor plan geometry, nearly 300 experimental stations are freely placed according to the program of curator Joe Ansel. From all directions, visitors are showered with sensations: lighting bolts strike through the darkened space, smoke and fumes are vented somewhere, loud noises clang in yet another direction. The typical video projections are, however, absent. The goal is, after all, promoting "understanding" in the sense of "grasping". The museum in Wolfsburg impresses visitors with its striking architecture. At the same time, building and presentation are in an ideal state of harmony. Here, the entire family can have fun, learn things, and be astonished while enjoying themselves. Even if the concept of the Science Center cannot be translated without much ado into other exhibition types, the Phaeno Museum can give an indication where we are headed when venturing through the realm of museums.

To exhibit – From the spoon to the state

Ruedi Baur

Let's start at the beginning, at the time and place where things received their purpose, where their origin is. And let's ask the basic questions: What qualifies an object for an exhibition? And what is an exhibition anyway? The modern use of the term is still defined by the mindset of the era of enlightenment – the era of the great emancipation of the mind, which propagated rational thinking, challenged established authorities and thus ultimately provided the basis for a modern national consciousness. The great national museums were established back then. With their museographic logic they impressed people even more than the contemporary governmental and royal institutions could. What remains of this idea in the era of globalization and a concept of nation that has been artificially revived in the Western world, disoriented by and since September 11th? Can we really speak of a transformation of the art of exhibiting? Which contradictions is the newly developed discipline of scenography subject to today, which had its glory days in the last decade of the past century? What purpose do contemporary exhibitions serve anyway? According to which concepts are exhibitions developed and created, and by whom? What do the diverse stakeholders expect from the various temporary and permanent exhibitions?

Far from answering all questions here, it does seem necessary however to look at the origin of the act of exhibiting beyond the first national museums in order to understand our current point of view. In short, we will attempt to remember, understand, and interpret current motivations of both exhibition makers and also exhibition visitors. Some claim that "everything can be exhibited today." Should digitizing of information and dematerialization of consumption indeed lead to an obsession of conservation, we are fortunately confronted with the realization that everything, in fact, can't be exhibited anymore.

However: Our so-called event societies, in their quest for the event for event's sake, are rediscovering particular aspects of the "monstrous" origin of the term of exhibiting once more. Does this mean the enlightening and educational demands are forgotten?

The title "To exhibit – From the spoon to the state" is of course reminiscent of the knowledge and experience demanded by Max Bill[1] in particular, and through him by these modern designer-architects who thought that they alone were capable of understanding the totality of constitutive elements of our society, from the minuscule everyday object to the gigantic city of the future.

Correspondingly, the scenographers' task is to design this "second world", in which the (re-) presentation of objects of everyday life and abstract, undefined ideas such as the nation are made visible simultaneously. However, what becomes apparent is that exhibitions differ significantly in their conceptual approach. Contrary to the proposed goal of directly illustrating a subject by presenting a collection of objects, particular contemporary exhibitions don't even use the object anymore for demonstrating their subject. Thus, e.g. an idea can be exhibited under the same label as objects. Beyond their topical premise, the various ways of presentation facilitate highly diverse exhibitions: from the museum of local history via the famous international exhibitions to exhibitions that write history, those that proudly tell of science and technology, those that present the extraordinary and ordinary aspects of our and other societies, or display works of art to be seen and understood, and many more. All of these different forms of exhibiting equally and indirectly show the sometimes difficult relationship between form and content, or without intending to simplify this topic, between conservators and scenographers. However, we would like to focus on the difficult causative question of "why". Let us begin with analyzing the word "exhibition" itself.

Exhibition/exposition/expositium/monstra/Ausstellung/...

In our case, the method of analyzing translations of a term proves particularly insightful. The most interesting little variations become apparent when researching the words "exhibition" and "to exhibit" in various languages. In analyzing their different origins, these seemingly trivial words permit a scholarly way of reading. In those languages that I am familiar with there are quite a number of additional expressions such as "to present the eye", "to open a view", "to publicly display", "to showcase", "to perform an act of exhibitionism", "to reclaim from the shadows", "to lay out", "to come into view", ... All of these are pervaded by connotations of pedestal, frame, illumination, and explanation. What becomes obvious is the difference between the time of nameless and inaccessible storage, of collection, and gathering – and the time of illumination in which a chosen object is either detached from its common use, or retrieved from its 100-year sleep, the depth of the depot, vault, and storage room.

Slow down please! In all of these expressions, neither the object or in fact the observer is pronouncedly expressed as being present. Latter contains terminology that, in almost none of these languages, actually relates to the term of

2

3

4

exhibiting. The visitors/visiteurs/visitatores/Besucher are confronted, in their visual visitations, with elements that have been brought into the light. This double origin is noticeable where it relates to the observer and where, in more distinguished terms, it relates to the visitor.

Showing things/ostentation and other exhibition types
But not only the visitor, also the objects as stated above are missing in the analyzed terminology. One only needs to take a look at those hideous colonialist exhibitions in order to understand that this absence is created by denial. At the same time, next to exotic products, exotic objects are put on display: The "domesticated noble savage" and even the entire concept of controlling "savage peoples" embodied by the "good white Christian European colonizer" comprise the spotlight, pedestal, and adornment of recontextualization.

What follows now is the term of the dramatized concept. Thus, we dedicate our interest to the parading of the living body. It allows us to transcend the obstacle of our beautifying glance in order to trace a potential and possible origin of the term exhibition. Three scenes come to mind: Firstly the slave market, then executions and other public acts of executing sentences, and finally the almost trivial hustle and bustle on the festival markets of times past. Everything there was for sale, yet at the same time another kind of dramatization developed, in comparison only intended for the purpose of exhibiting objects. Side by side with the most sensational objects, paraded as shamelessly as possible, one could find the most horrible human abnormalities, animals, and presumably "wild" creatures that were put on display in a pitiful state of imprisonment.[2] In all three cases, our previously noted definitions are confirmed. They obviously are retrieved from the dungeon, from the obscured depths of inaccessibility, from the realm of darkness, in order to create this event by parading the creatures of damnation before a public lusting for sensation. Even if the discipline of scenography discussed here prefers to consider the stage and the limelight as its origin, it seems more appropriate to me to trace this origin within the satisfaction of a pathological voyeurism. The English term "exhibition" by the way indeed retains the memory of this forced exhibitionism and its ability to arouse the mob.

I demand on inclusion of this dimension with some insistence, perhaps out of fear that macabre populists might arise again within this discipline. Particular intentions are alarming to me that luckily pertain to a vanishing minority among my colleagues, also particular fascinations, scenographic excesses, ignorance towards displayed content, particular agreeable compromises. Scenographers should prove resistant to sponsors' harmful appeals. Let us not forget that all power that is based on lie and authority can develop a significant energy for dramatizing a process of devotion and belief. After significantly influencing culture at the end of the past century, scenographers are now in the process of returning to this conflict of dramatizing leadership and power, to the creation of events for events sake. The marketing ideology that controls our societies, weary of consumption, has undeniably and obviously discovered the power of seduction that radiates from this equipment of narrative space and from its ability to artificially create brand identity. Attracted by astronomical budgets – while funding for culture is further drastically cut – some within the discipline leave the traditional museums and their educational purposes in order to contribute to trade shows[3], supermarkets, luxury hotels, or other pseudo-museums for the promotion of major international brands. By the way, a need for great sensations capable of filling the incredible void within a part of the public, stuck between ever increasing desire and frustration due to excessive consumption, is indeed noticeable. Intoxicated by the success of their accomplishments, sponsors and creative class dig deeper. Thus, the scenographer, despite a particular formal restraint and sometimes very successful pseudo-cultural camouflage, feels happy in this market of extraordinary exhibitions, the only goal of which is to induce sheer surprise and lucid admiration, in short, a free event. Yet is this really as free as it seems?

Representations and other clarifications

Let's take a look at the opposite case. Departing from the fascination of sensation we reach its radical counterpart: knowledge transfer. In regard to this concept, we remind ourselves of one of its significant drivers in historic terms, the long and difficult path to secularization, as well as the equally difficult and still ongoing process of citizens and their representatives taking political power into their own hands. The battle against the different manifestations of obscurantism and propaganda was taken on by making phenomena understood, i. e. by explanation, plausibility, sharing knowledge, enlightening. This goal could never be reached without at least trying to be credible. For this to happen, knowledge required official confirmation, on the one hand by general accessibility and on the other by monumentalizing presentation spaces in which knowledge transfer could take place.

At this point it seems necessary to me – in order to avoid the simplifying patterns of dialectics – to take a look at how people understand the act of exhibiting. In the case of the event we have seen that the emphasis is generally rather on what the English more fittingly call entertainment. Particular people thus talk of lulling the citizen and consumer, of filling the all-encompassing void by artificially triggered emotions, of new religions that replace the old ones and feed off the transfer of individual and collective emotions. In order to function permanently and also be credible, this event-related approach needs to include at least a minimum of content. Just as, in return, the intention to provide knowledge requires at least a minimum effort in dramatization.

But let's take a closer look at the origin of the exhibition and the museum in classic republicanism in France. As we have seen, the word "exhibition" means to make something accessible to the public eye, to make something visible in an explanatory way. However, during the century of the enlightenment, in which this act of exhibiting in the context of classic republicanism was established, this intention wasn't always as obvious. Simultaneously, the question of distribution arises, for instance simply how to use the wealth that the

5

6

1   Crystal Palace, London 1851; Joseph Paxton
    Exhibition building for the first World Fair. Photograph, ca. 1900
2   Professor Palmer's office – medical stage show, ca. 1860
3   Slave market, Richmond, Virginia, USA. Wood carving, 1861
4   Market in Kashgar, Xinjiang Province, China
5   Villagio Mall, Doha, Qatar. The mall is the Middle East's largest.
6   Indonesian, traditional attire, Mall of Jakarta

7

8

royal families had amassed. Destroy, pillage, distribute? These primary revolutionary instincts were quickly supplanted by the invention of the museum of classic republicanism – a surrogate both for conservation as well as a testimony of a past that was mummified by the museographic act. By dramatizing an outdated past, people simply become aware of how different it is from their own present and future. Is it any different today?

One thing is certain; it was a mistake to exclusively focus on destroying the past. The goal always was and still is the construction of a collective "we" centered around the shared revolutionary past, without talking about how knowledge transfer makes people aware of their responsibilities. By the way, each of these two points of view has developed their own museographic forms. Whereas the first is elevated on top of a pedestal, into a frame, and into a monument, the second in particular expresses itself via explanations and experiments. The first approach leads to the great national museums, the national, international, and global exhibitions. The second however creates the museums of the humans, natural science and natural historic museums, scientific and technological, historic and ethnological exhibitions and museums. Some of them are clearly directed towards the great illuminated bourgeois public, others towards a specialized audience,[4] yet all of them are intended to demonstrate the public benefit of art and knowledge.

To summarize we can say that exhibition concepts can differ in fundamental ways even if the methods used may, in specific cases, seem very similar. The role of scenographers is directly related to this. It seems important to me that they are capable of distinguishing between the relevant requirements that the purpose of representation, the culture of entertainment, the desire for sensation call for – or, in reverse – that the transfer of knowledge demands; not to forget the economical aspects, especially available time for leisure and culture. In many cases, these requirements overlap in highly contradictory ways. However, sponsors do not directly address them. With the help of a few fictitious examples we can attempt to demonstrate the interrelation between exhibition design and its dramatization.

The spoon exhibition
We could, mind you, also choose a different object. This little instrument of our every-day life however permits conducting the following exercise. It begins with demonstrating the logical relationships between content and formal requirements. Of course, every case can be formulated in one way or another. I prefer schematic approaches that occur repeatedly.

Example 1: A manufacturer of small spoons wants to show his expert knowledge, as well as the extraordinary design, the product value, and indirectly the brand he is responsible for in an exhibition.
The character of the exhibition is in danger of being too serious yet is innovative in general and has an air of restrained modernism. The intention here is to exhibit the object according to its true value. It is elevated from its triviality and provided a higher symbolic value by being brought into connection with this particular brand and its long corporate tradition of manufacturing know-how, or the reputation of the designer

who in fact designed it. The dramatization is generated by a process in which the transmission of symbols confirms the object's true value. The object itself is irrelevant, as it is sold in large quantities and distributed worldwide. It doesn't have to be on display in larger numbers since consumers can consider their own purchase as something special. The spoon is displayed with the importance of a unique specialty. The entire scenographic art consists of turning the trivial into something exceptional without letting this magic appear too obvious. The presentation of the conceptualization and manufacturing process and, even more so, the symbolic quality of the creators provide the object with its necessary dose of history. Thus, the spoon, detached from its typical context of use, can be put on display. The focus is however on the aspects that provide this valorization, yet without pedestal or frame, as the spoon is to remain accessible. The scenography depends on the promotional strategy.

9

Example 2: The presentation of an ensemble of small spoons from a collection.

As opposed to the previous case, every single piece is relevant here. The scenography helps visitors appreciate the appearance of each individual object. This way, differences can easily be compared and comprehended. The individual object is placed in relation to an ensemble. The intention is to emphasize its uniqueness and true value. The exhibition visitors descend into a darkened room where they can concentrate on the illuminated exhibit. A written or verbal explanation supports the exhibit. Its restrained appearance prevents distracting viewers from the object on display. The most exceptional pieces of the collection are separated from the ensemble and presented individually. A verbal or visual message is required to explain this selection. A good idea is to introduce the collector at the end of the exhibition and describe his passion for collecting. The exhibition piece is in the focus of attention. Thus, an installation that is too expressive may render content illegible. As result, the scenography is oriented on appearance. It withdraws behind the content, and by doing so provides for good legibility of the idea.

10

Example 3: The presentation of the special little spoon from the collection of illustrious people of note.

Similar to the first example, this is sort of an over-representation. Expressing the exceptional quality of this spoon calls for adding an artificial symbolic component to the exhibit. For this purpose, either a particular piece of information or a dramaturgic effect can be emphasized. Demonstrating the connection between the spoon and the symbolic added value needs to confirm the exceptional quality of the exhibited object, trivial as such. Considering how ridiculous the situation is, the installation will definitely be powerfully expressive, perhaps even self-ironic. A good presentation idea will cover up the weak content.

7 State visit of the Vice President of Cyprus to the Federal Republic of Germany, sightseeing of the treasure chamber, Munich Residence, 1963
8 British Museum, London, 1848; Robert Smirke
The origin of the museum is a private collection that the state received as gift in 1753. The building was one of the first that was exclusively built for the purpose of presenting a collection to the public.
9 Silver spoon collection, second hand market
10 The Chamber of Crafts emphasizes special quality by exhibiting exemplary apprentice and journeyman's pieces. Berlin, 1930
11 Irina Troitskaya's private spoon collection

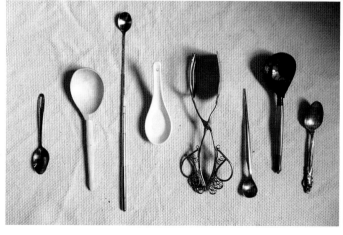

11

Example 4: Ethnological research on how this instrument is used in different cultures.
In this case, the special quality of each object is of maximum interest. However, in contrast to the previous example, the spoon is only the pretext; an introduction to dealing with more comprehensive social and societal questions. The spoon permits us to digress from the subject and deal with diverse developments, yet also return to the original question with each new chapter. In a certain way, this question represents the refrain of the exhibition. The exhibition piece demonstrates the difference in use and knowledge that may develop within different media. The temporal and geographic dimensions establish the totality; and only the subject in its totality can generate an understanding of the interrelationships between the different objects and their uses. The evidence that the exhibition visitor encounters on his roundtrip can however be presented in highly different ways. Yet, the dramaturgy needs to fully complement the content of the exhibition. It emphasizes its message by enabling the visitor to experience it without simulating it. Here we come full circle with the transfer of knowledge and the question how interest can be generated without simultaneously trivializing the operation. It is recommended to permit different levels of immersion in the narrative structure of the exhibition. The scenography is required to enable this legibility to differing degrees. It will be successful if reading each statement does not obstruct the legibility of the whole. The visitor shall always have the freedom to experience the exhibition independently.

Example 5: The interpretation of a society based on the spoon as evidence for the level of development of a society. This is comparable to the fourth example, except from the fact that it may be interesting to illustrate the cases of doubt – what may be unknown – in order to avoid an all too contemporary and all too European perspective. This would be possible via a dramaturgy of astonishment – for instance by showing a whole lot of spoons instead of a single one. In this case, imagination is necessary to relive a moment of the past. Attempts at hyperrealism are seldom successful. Scenographers have to recognize again and again that they are dealing with a hypothesis, a scientific theater. Focusing on one particular sense of perception may enable creating a connection, however contradictory, between reinstatement and conservation of doubt. For instance, the ambience of a past society can be experienced by displaying the spoon alone or by creating an atmosphere that triggers the imagination by avoiding false assumptions. At this point I might as well discuss the concept of virtual space in which visitors move. The relationship between body, space, and information is central to all exhibitions (ill. 13).[5] However, the audio-visual has already introduced significant aspects of time and movement into the exhibition space. The virtual, interactive space is suitable for permitting the visitor to design his own way within a virtual world. His body is present; the space reacts to this presence, however within defined parameters. Touching the spoon can, for instance, activate particular ele-

12 "Elvis' last Cadillac", Elvis-Presley-Museum, St. Margarethen.
    For special commemoration, personal objects become museum exhibits.
13 Herbert Bayer, diagram: "extended field of vision", 1935
14 Army exhibition, Thun, 2006
    Exhibition of Swiss Army bivouac fabric. A spoon is on display representing soldiers' personal equipment.

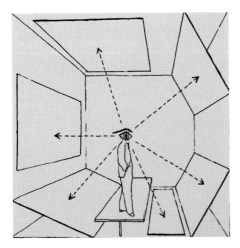

ments within the space. The touched object thus will connect the virtual with the real. Experience however shows that this mode of presentation suppresses its content and, in general, fascinates the observer more through its technology than by the content it mediates. This is more or less a spatial experiment, the content of which is merely a pretext, rather than actually representing content. However, the appropriate use of this method and inclusion thereof needs to be based on thorough research.

Example 6: An installation dealing with the culinary arts. In this case, the spoon is nothing more than a pretext and a supporting element for the presentation of different ingredients. We can imagine the setting of the installation without difficulty. The diversity and amount of objects amplifies the dramaturgy. The ensemble can be seen as a totality; here, differences can be experienced in sequence. 2000 spoons and 2000 little monitors displaying chewing mouths, 2000 recipes and images of extraordinary dishes. The exhibition can be viewed in two minutes or alternately enjoyed for hours and hours. The dramaturgy is however the central focus, on which the message completely relies.

Exhibiting the state
We now move on from objects to more abstract ideas. What is a nation, a state? Certainly, a territory, a population, an administrative and political structure, a government – but also a history, an economy, a culture, one or more languages, a national soccer team, borders – the combination of these elements. All of this seems as equally abstract as globalization, international networks, voluntary and forced migrations, tourism, global information, the dissolution of borders. The accumulation of structures makes these ideas difficult to read and renders them completely artificial. For more than a century do states invest incredible funds for presenting themselves to themselves and to the rest of the world at the same time. National, international, and world exhibitions, topical exhibitions of all kinds follow one another in a fixed rhythm established in almost one and a half centuries. Complicated competitions between nations that, through proximity of their pavilions, suddenly become comparable. Here and there, all of this seems rather pointless, but the ritual is perpetuated and continues happily ever after from one exhibition to the next. Absence seems impossible.
We'll assume that this exhibiting of states is just another simple example. This way we can analyze exhibitions, the subjects of which are much more complex and abstract than simple object-oriented exhibitions. Similar to the spoon we will describe a number of fictitious examples and will attempt to imagine scenographic gestures. Indeed, a world exposition permits comparing often highly different approaches to presentation. The challenge is to attract more visitors than anyone else. Of course, credibility also plays a role, and – behind the scenes – business, plain and simple. Here as well as elsewhere, the detrimental ideologies of branding and marketing have begun to exert their influence. Nations are sold as a product just as the tableware we just analyzed. We shall return to this, but let's begin with the more self-evident approaches.

Example 1: Presentation of a certain number of values that characterize a nation.
Before we begin: Here, just as in all other examples, the

pavilion architecture is an active component of scenography. One can consider the exhibition as a totality that begins with approaching the building and even with the media presence of the event before that. Then, the following questions arise: Which message does the building communicate? How do you enter the building? How welcome are visitors? How do you feel there? Are visitors accepted as independent individuals in their own right? Does the whole thing make any sense at all? To which degree does the appearance appear to be ephemeral or permanent? Does public perception match the intentions of sponsors and scenographers? Latter will have to answer these questions in any case, as their perceptions significantly influence an exhibition visit and its message as well. The task is to simultaneously maintain content, shell, and function, and to coordinate architects, scenographers, and those responsible for the function within a collaborative team. And to accept at the same time that it is the combination of all these aspects that conveys values; and in doing so it has to be ensured that these values are consistent throughout. Before we continue, we perhaps need to take a closer look at the question of values. The expression may seem problematic, knowing that it usually is abused for reactionary purposes. Certainly, the dictatorships of the 20th century as well as authoritarian democracies have deliberately employed such exhibitions and attempted to communicate the sentiments of strength attributed to their regimes. But beyond that, other more positive values can be communicated by the architecture and scenography: human rights, ecological awareness or simply wellbeing, restraint, acknowledging citizens as political beings, cosmopolitanism, openness, modernity, etc. In other words, each visitor who enters such a pavilion has a certain image of the represented country in their minds. The question is which relationship exists between this image and the pavilion's message. It will be easily possible for the one to confirm the other. However, in this case it is important that these elements are perceived as positive. It is more difficult to provide for continued evolution of the original image even if it corresponds to reality. Knowing that exhibitions are a means for immersion of the visitor within this ideal image that has the power to correct preconceived images, nations utilize this means brazenly. In its best cases the positive qualities of a country, its diversity, and even its imperfection can be demonstrated. In its worst cases these means are used for propaganda, or in a more contemporary version used for the creation of fictitious images – the new system of politically correct propaganda, currently known as branding. Whichever the approach and intention may be, luckily visitors are more or less capable of decoding them, both in regard to the vision and the perception of the pavilion and its function, and in regard to the exhibition content. Furthermore, the question arises whether the exhibition serves its purpose. Is it imaginable that the pavilion as such conveys the values of a nation by employing similar structures and interrelations? Even if the presentation perhaps shows signs of bias, it is insightful to treat the exhibition simply as entering a building that is capable of communicating itself as this value system.

15 World Fair, Paris, 1900
   view across the Seine towards the Street of Nations
16 Indian temple, Colonial Exhibition, Paris 1931
17 Exhibition, "German people – German labor", Berlin, 1934
   Leuna-Werke, partial view, chemistry department

Example 2: The values as such are commonplace, yet are simultaneously communicated through a topical exhibition. This is the most frequent case. The architecture has its own language that, in better cases, is partially incorporated into the exhibition. The exhibition deals with a given topic and thus attempts to display the values and potentials of a country. It is easily perceived that the subject is often only a pretext for the ulterior motives of representation and persuasion. The scenographer should not be under any illusions. Throughout the conceptual process he will be limited to his factual role of setting the stage for a nation. Due to limited available space here we can't discuss some of the successful experiments and even less so the many failures. It will remain for independent historians to reveal the relationship between the conceptual process these pavilions are based on and their failure. This would be very important indeed to prevent committing the same mistakes over and over again.

Example 3: The nation represents itself through one of its representatives.[6]
To me, this solution seems among the best – if independence is guaranteed to a certain degree – in order to prevent an exhibition that is devoid of interest, full of compromises, trivially event-driven, miserably populist and coarsely propaganda-oriented. If this representative were himself a scenographer or would collaborate with one, then these authors could represent particular characteristics and reflect reality in a much better way than the nation itself. The freer they are, the more credible they can be. By choosing the authors, the nation demonstrates restraint and respect for the opinions of free and independent political citizens.

Example 4: The nation represents itself through the knowledge and experience of its corporations.
Since nation-states have unfortunately been significantly weakened by economic liberalism, they often prefer to give voice to those who are willing and capable of sponsoring the event. However, these are the people whose businesses profit from the exhibition. In this case, one indirectly becomes visitor of a trade show with a subliminal commercial objective, more or less subtly cloaked by superfluous verbiage. The whole thing completely loses its appeal.

Example 5: The nation expresses its diversity, its character, its reality.
This direction is currently losing its verve due to the ideological rule of marketing that promotes limiting things to the bare essential. It seems to me however that this direction corresponds best to a democratic value system. How should the rich diversity of a country be expressed without simultaneously sacrificing the powerful correlation of a message? In this case, the art of exhibiting newly comes into play; perhaps even through one of its origins: the market, with its ability to express diversity in an expansive context. What could a credible dramaturgy look like, capable of providing a collection of differences that illustrate the entire wealth of the cosmopolitism of contemporary societies? Perhaps we have to give up the nation as such and simply focus on continents or even simpler, cities, in which more than 50% of the world's population live today and which permit this diversity and represent it.

And the city?
Returning to Max Bill's original phrase "from the spoon to the city", not to the state, we conclude with proposing exhibitions outside of the established framework of the museum or the conventional exhibition space, these "white boxes" that automatically neutralize the exhibit or the exhibition concept and detach it from its context. We can imagine an exhibition within urban space and its resulting dramatization, or even better, making this habitat legible. Certainly, the idea isn't new; the experiment has already been conducted, especially in the world of contemporary art. However, these dramatizations, translated from exhibition culture, include the intrinsic contradictory factors of this discipline: the sensational, the representative, the enlightening. Which will persist, and how can they join in harmony? Such subjects and questions will certainly motivate architects and scenographers for time to come.

1   Bill, Max: Die gute Form. Winterthur 1957. Max Bill intended to create objects and places that were supposed to be a model for aspects of everyday life, in his own words, "from the spoon to the city".
2   Pastoureau, Michel: Der Bär. Geschichte eines gestürzten Königs. Neu-Isenburg 2008. Pastoureau illustrates the humiliating exhibition of the captured and dishonored mythical animal.
3   Koolhaas, Rem: Delirious New York. A Retroactive Manifesto for Manhattan. London 1978
4   As e. g. the well-known Musée du Monuments Français in Paris, a sculptures museum which had been initiated by the architect Viollet-le Duc. It includes a collection of scale models of the most important French monuments. The goal was to create awareness for renovation and for this purpose establish various professional associations. The museum has been renovated since and is called Cité de l'Architecture et du Patrimoine today.
5   Bayer, Herbert: Diagram extended field of vision, 1935. In: Herbert Bayer: Visual Communication Architecture Painting. New York 1967
6   This is often the case, e. g. in the Art and Architecture Biennale in Venice. The national pavilions present the works of an artist who also serves as exhibition designer at the same time.

Image selection: Christine Dorothee Schwienhorst

17

Phaeno Science Center in Wolfsburg

Architects: Zaha Hadid Architects, London;
Mayer Bährle Freie Architekten, Lörrach
Exhibition design: Ansel Associates, Point Richmond

Site plan
scale 1:5,000

This spectacular experimentation landscape invites visitors to explore natural and technological phenomena with all senses of perception.

The Phaeno Science Center is located in the city center of Wolfsburg, directly next to the train station, terminating the Porschestrasse. The area, long neglected by urban planning, features buildings predominantly from the 1950s and 1960s. Within this heterogeneous environment, the science center's sculptural architecture lets it stand out, redefines the train station plaza, and creates another attraction for the Autostadt on the other side of the Mittelland channel. The chunky building structure of exposed concrete, measuring 154 m in length and 80 m in width, is supported by ten conical volumes of different dimensions, the so-called "cones". The publicly accessible space beneath the building is reminiscent of a flowing landscape with caves and grottos.

Experimental stations for various topics
The "cones" accommodate various functions such as restaurant, bar, Phaeno-shop, auditorium, and entrance. An escalator provides access to the experimentation landscape situated 7 m above ground level. Here as well, a monochrome environment of bulges, waves, and curves produces a futuristic interior landscape. Stairs and doorways flow seamlessly into floors and transform into balustrades and floor bumps.

The 9,000 m² exhibition area features approximately 300 experimentation stations conceived by Ansel Associates. The JoinIn stations, demonstration experiments, and exhibits may be roughly arranged according to the topics of wind and weather, light and vision, movement, energy and matter, information, games, micro and macro. However, there is no planned, strict succession. The intention is rather that visitors explore the landscape on their own and trace phenomena of natural science and technology with all senses of perception. Contrary to the architecture with its restrained white and grey color selection, the stations are designed in a mostly very colorful way. In the three JoinIn laboratories, visitors can delve further into the subject matter of the experimentation stations.

Special construction
The concrete sculpture, created with significant effort and seemingly having no right angle, was only possible by using self consolidating concrete, a recent innovation in construction. The structure provided another challenge for the engineers involved. The building is solely supported by the ten "cones". As opposed to what would be considered normal, they are placed on their tip, and not on their bottom, seemingly illogical. Their supporting cross section decreases while the load increases, and as result stress within these members rises disproportionately. The ceiling above the ground level, simultaneously floor of the exhibition level, is comprised of a lattice structure that distributes loads equally in all directions, necessary due to the different shapes and placement of the supporting cones and the resulting ever changing main load direction. A spliced Vierendeel steel structure spans across the column-free exhibition area. The structure consists of parallel beams running in two directions, however intersecting at individual, different angles.

Project data:

Use:	culture/education
Museum/collection type:	technology/natural science museum
Construction:	reinforced concrete
Gross footprint:	12,631 m²
Exhibition area:	7,000 m²
Construction cost:	€ 79 million (gross)
Completion:	2005
Construction time:	39 months

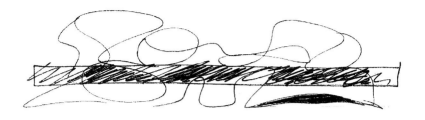

Section · floor plans
scale 1:2,000

1 Main entrance
2 Group entrance
3 Shop
4 Bistro/restaurant
5 Auditorium
6 Forum for ideas
7 Café/bar
8 Laboratory
9 "Terrace of innovation"
10 "Weather kitchen"
11 "Walk of life"
12 "Display of energy"
13 "Sound cave"
14 "Plateau of vision"
15 Administration

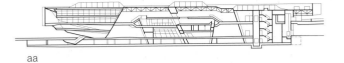

aa

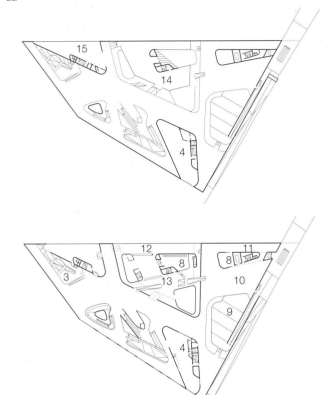

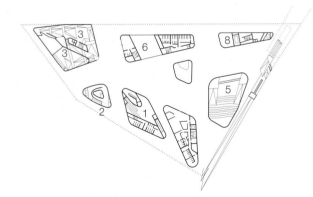

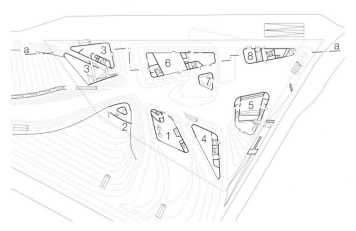

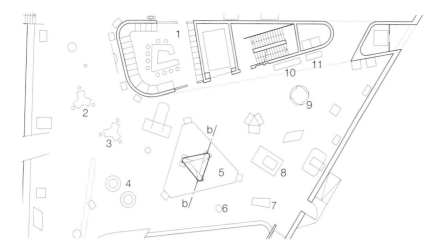

Partial floor plan, "Weather kitchen" area
scale 1:400

1 "LifeLab": chemical and biological laboratory
2 Microscope station including live specimens
3 Stereo microscope with various specimens
4 "Geyser"
5 "Stella": projections and experiments on climate
6 "Fog chamber": illustrates how fog develops
7 "Ball in the air stream": how does flying work?
8 "Air gun": production of air turbulence
9 "Fog tornado"
10 "Warm front": displays development of atmospheric layers and weather
11 "Seasons and the sun": why are there seasons?

Vertical section
"Stella" station
scale 1:20

12 aluminum flooring panel, embossed 6 mm
13 base plate steel sheet metal,
     powder coated 12 mm
14 steel sheet metal casing, powder coated
     3 mm, including ventilation feed-through
15 wood composite material, tinted 12 mm
16 console, HPL plywood
     light grey finish 5 mm
17 monitor (removable for
     maintenance purposes)
18 wood composite panel,
     grey-blue laminate 38 mm,
     white laminate in projection area

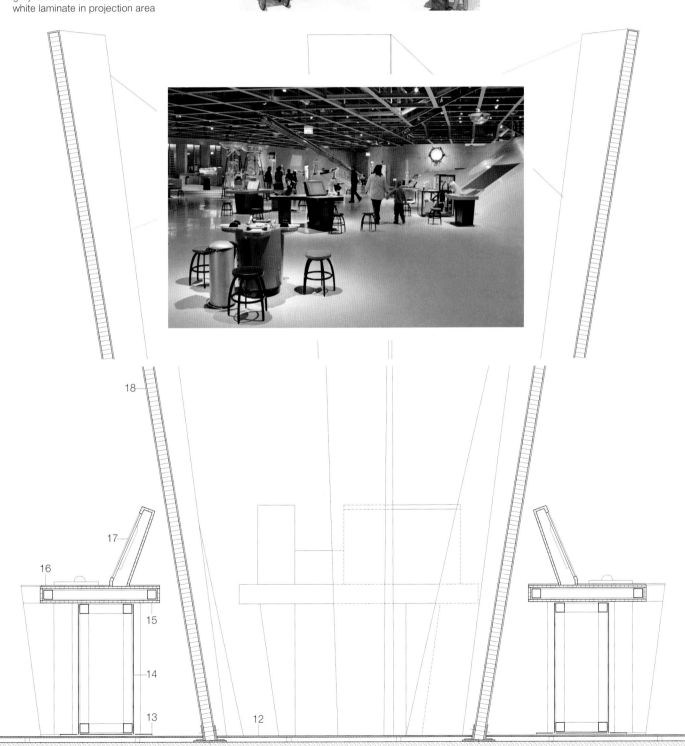

bb

New Museum in New York

Architects: SANAA/Kazuyo Sejima + Ryue Nishizawa, Tokyo

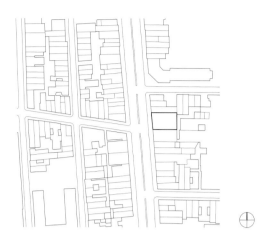

Six differently proportioned boxes, stacked one onto the other, serve as neutral presentation rooms for the exhibits.

Located in the Bowery, a quarter in Manhattan's south with a distinct subcultural character, the New Museum is visible from afar. The tower, comprised of offset cubes, is 53 m tall and thus exceeds neighboring buildings in height, on a plot that is only 20 m wide. Having changed its location a number of times, the museum, dedicated to contemporary art and founded in 1977, has moved into this new building, specifically tailored to its needs. Due to the limited width of the site, the extensive program is distributed vertically across nine levels. From the entrance level with ticket counter, museum shop, café and a small exhibition area located in the rear of the building, visitors can reach the auditorium downstairs or the three exhibition levels upstairs. The education center is located on the fourth floor, the administration offices further above, as well as an event space with adjoining terrace and building utilities on the top floors. The arrangement of the six stacked boxes with their different heights creates a rhythmic division within the building structure and adds to its fragmented appearance. Moreover, the stacking makes different uses become visible on the exterior.

On the three gallery levels, skylights are created through the offset arrangement of boxes, each oriented in a different direction. The individual boxes enable experiencing the interior through the different proportions of spaces. Their convergence point is the building core with staircase and elevator. The steel structure on the interior side of the facade permits column-free, flexible gallery spaces. Grey polished concrete floors and white walls create presentation spaces with neutral character, and exposed ceilings emphasize their slightly rough appearance.

Expanded aluminum shell

A metallic skin homogeneously covers the building and emphasizes the individual cube volumes. Depending on the direction of daylight, this skin appears solid as a sculpture, and sometimes light as fabric. The expanded metal facade consists of altogether 988 elements at 2,133 mm × 2,895 mm each. In order to make the façade appear as seamless as possible, the overlap of individual elements measures 25 mm; at the same time, this provides tolerances for assembly. Stainless steel connectors fix the expanded metal panels at a distance of 76 mm to the corrugated sheet aluminum facade surface, thus giving the impression of floating in front of the facade.

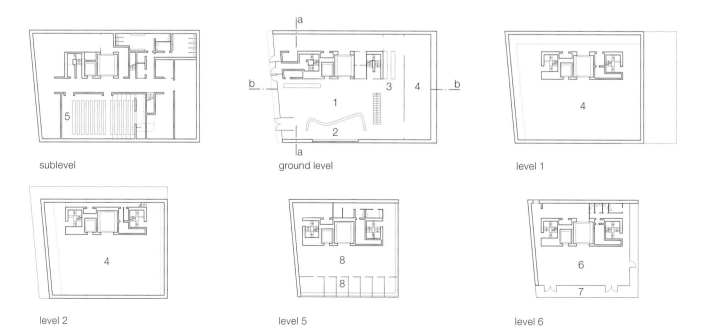

sublevel

ground level

level 1

level 2

level 5

level 6

Project Data:

Use:	cultural/education
Museum Type:	museum for contemporary art
Construction:	reinforced concrete
Clear room height:	5.5–7.31 m (exhibition areas)
Footprint:	5,453 m²
Exhibition area:	1,217 m²
Completion:	2007
Construction time:	24 months

Site plan
scale 1:5,000
Floor plans · sections
scale 1:750

1 Entrance lobby
2 Museum shop
3 Café
4 Exhibition
5 Theater/auditorium
6 Multiple use space
7 Roof terrace
8 Administration
9 Utilities
10 Education center

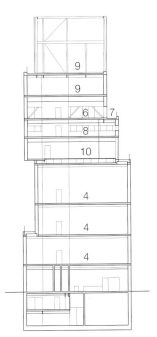

aa

bb

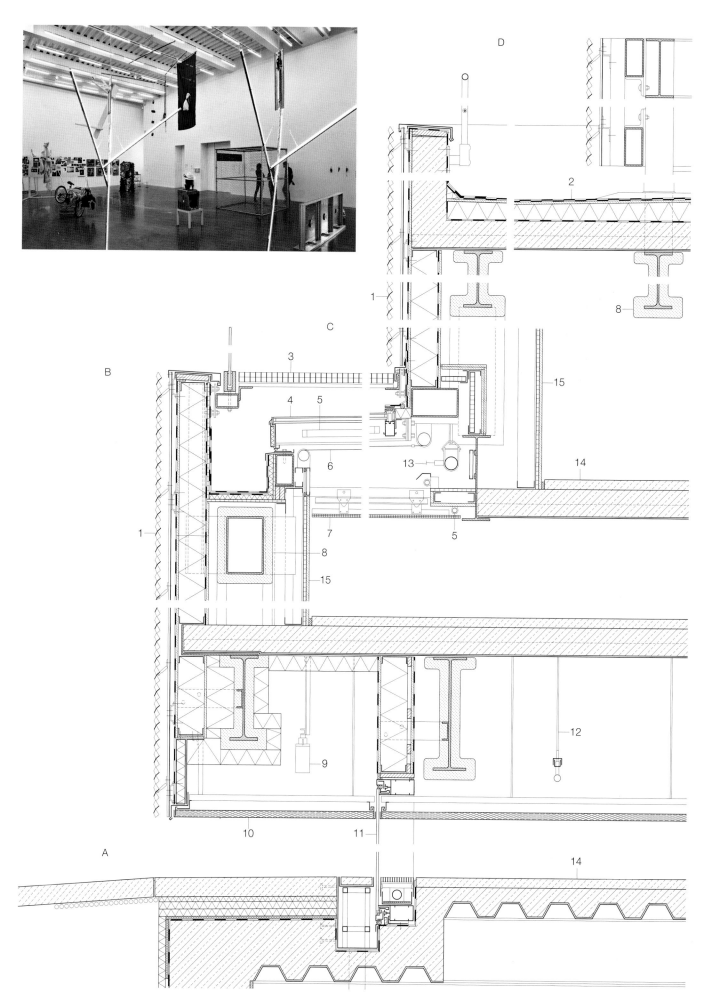

D

2

1

8

C

B

3

4   5

6

13

15

1

5

14

1

8

15

I

I

9

12

10   11

A

14

Vertical section
Scale 1:20

1 wall construction:
   aluminum expanded metal panels, anodized
   3 mm, panel size 2,133.6/2,895.6/38 mm
   stainless steel connectors
   corrugated extruded aluminum panels
   rib width 13 mm
   ventilation space 24 mm
   diffusion open wind barrier
   F 90 fireproof gypsum board 16 mm
   metal stud framing
   mineral fiber insulation 140 mm
   vapor barrier
   F 90 fireproof gypsum board 16 mm

2 roof terrace:
   bituminous roofing, 2 layers 5.6 mm
   white PVC aggregate
   composite gypsum board,
   water-resistant 13 mm
   insulation 140–100 mm
   bituminous layer 2.3 mm
   reinforced concrete composite floor/
   ceiling 159 mm
   metal decking 76 mm
3 maintenance access,
   metal grating 50 mm
4 skylight, security glass 6 mm + 16 mm air
   space + 2× 5 mm laminated glass
   with dot-pattern surface print 20 %
5 fluorescent strip lighting
6 textile sun protection

7 polycarbonate board 16 mm
8 steel construction with fireproofing
9 exterior lighting
10 suspended ceiling:
   aluminum expanded metal panels
   steel framing
11 clear laminate glass 19 mm
   anodized aluminum frame
12 suspension for fluorescent strip lighting
   steel rod ⌀ 5 mm
13 sprinkler unit
14 polished concrete 51 mm, reinforced
   concrete composite floor/ceiling 159 mm
   metal decking 76 mm
15 stucco painted white 3 mm
   gypsum board 16 mm, plywood board 16 mm
   metal stud framing

Literature Museum in Marbach

Architects: David Chipperfield Architects, London/Berlin
Exhibition design: Gestaltungsbüro element, Basle

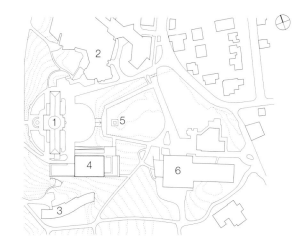

For the delicate exhibits of the literature archive the architects created visually calm rooms of varying proportions.

A better place for a literature museum other than Marbach is hardly imaginable, considering the tranquil town along the Neckar River had been a renowned literature location for some time. In 1759 Friedrich Schiller was born here, and in 1903 the Schiller National Museum was established on a hill at the outskirts of town to honor him. Within the course of time, this facility developed into a national institution: The German Literature Archive, on location since 1973 with its own library and administrative buildings.

This ensemble was complemented by the Modern Literature Museum, in short LiMo, by David Chipperfield Architects. The inventory consisting of literature of the 20th and 21st century finally can be put on display here; treasures that had been hidden in depots due to lack of appropriate exhibition rooms. As if it had been standing there all along, the new building fits naturally into the surrounding environment, infused with history: A temple-like pavilion in front of the grand Neckar landscape, hiding the largest part of its volume within the slope and inviting people to stroll about and sojourn along its surrounding walkways and terraces.

The interior has nothing in common with an art museum: Where usually all-white spaces, flooded with daylight, serve to dramatize paintings or sculptures, the rooms of the literature museum, clad in dark tropical wood, focus completely on the sensitive exhibits within showcases which are displayed with 50 lux, at chilly 18 °C and an ambient humidity of constantly 50 %. Each of the six spaces, differing in proportion and room height and featuring artificial lighting, borders at least two rooms with access to natural daylight. These daylight loggias contribute to a complex and varied roundtrip through the museum spaces.

Project Data:

Use:	cultural/education
Museum Type:	inventory of the German Literature Archive, 20th and 21st century collection
Construction:	exposed concrete
Clear room height:	3.23–10.60 m
Gross volume:	20,100 m³
Gross footprint:	3,800 m²
Exhibition area:	1,100 m²
Total cost:	€ 11.8 million
Completion:	2006
Construction time:	27 months

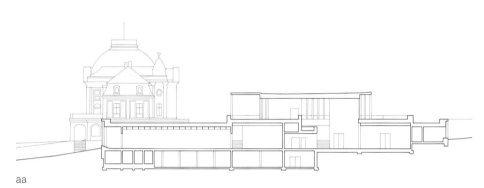

Site plan
scale 1:4,000
Section · floor plan
scale 1:800

1 Schiller National
  Museum
2 Administration
  and archive
3 Assembly building
4 Modern Literature
  Museum
5 Schiller Grove with
  Schiller Memorial
6 City hall
7 Archive
8 Auxiliary room
9 Storage
10 Temporary
   exhibition
11 Daylight loggia
12 Gallery
13 Lower foyer
14 Permanent
   exhibition
15 Terrace
16 Auditorium
17 Foyer with counter
   and wardrobe
18 Entrance

aa

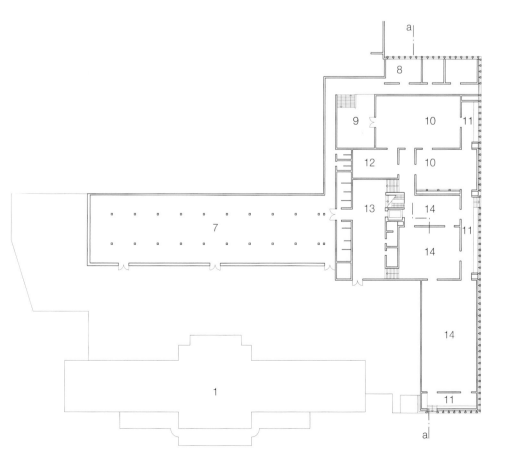

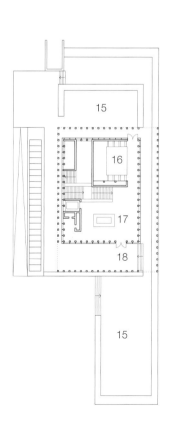

Fluxus, stylus, nexus – the exhibition spaces

The permanent exhibition in the Modern Literature Museum is based on a number of ambitious objectives: supporting the uniqueness of the architecture, its rough sensuality, and unpretentious modesty; making use of air, light, and shadow; respecting the inventory of the archive, sometimes hard to access, as exhibition objects, and to present them to the greater public in an all new light. Behind this all, another dream takes shape: showing how immersion in an aesthetic play with language, transcending every-day limitations, can occur.

Thus, the permanent exhibition is focused on three parts: the inventory of the Marbach archive (nexus), the literature inventory (stylus), and the exhibited moment of aesthetic experience (fluxus). Element, a design firm located in Basle, was responsible for implementing the concept. It was important to use as few as possible and as many as necessary means for designing the exhibition and guiding visitors. Each space can be easily comprehended in its employed method and can be surveyed at first glance. The instructional media are intended for visitors without any prior knowledge of the items on display. Within "nexus" (ill. 3), the task for creating an expansive, sensually impressive presentation of archive materials has been a great challenge for the designers. The exhibits are, despite supporting elements (fasteners, book holders, photo covers, signage), visible from all sides. They are placed on top of multiple glass layers, illuminated pane by pane. They invite visitors to move, to crouch, to stretch and to perceive things, perhaps also as an image if they are too far away for an in-depth reading – or to decipher them anyway with the help of the multimedia museum guide "M3", a kind of portable computer.

The three permanent exhibition spaces

Within the smallest space of the permanent exhibition, "fluxus" (ill. 2), prominent curators present their current personal literature selection: favorite books, unread texts, finds from their own archives. The 33 m² of the space can change in appearance according to individual curator's intentions: object, light, sound, or film space; dark room, cell, or cave; stage, scriptorium, library; projection surface for imagination. "Stylus" (ill. 1) places the substance of literature into the focus of attention: Signs, letters, words and wordings, writing styles, figures of speech and formulas of thought – all which can comprise the beauty of literature. The interactive installation, operating with various projections, provides an experi-

ence that can be compared to fishing. With the M3, visitors can catch letters like catching fish within the continuously moving sea of digits, moving according to no particular order. Visitors thus become fishermen of literary texts that however comprise a defined and not arbitrarily organized form.

The historic, mute, and immovable materials of the archive are in the center of "nexus": more than 1,300 exhibits – an almost negligible amount, compared to the more than 1,100 items from the estates of authors and scholars, more than 50 million single pages, 800,000 library units, and 200,000 art objects that are kept in Marbach at this time. The exhibition communicates with the archive; the selection of exhibits changes in the rhythm of its purchases and discoveries. The permanent exhibition of the archive inventory "nexus" inter-

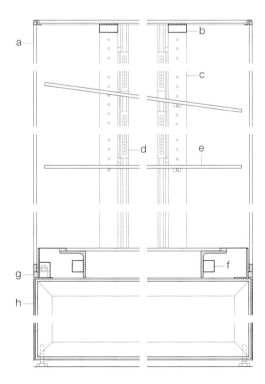

1 Exhibition space "stylus"
2 Exhibition space "fluxus"
3 Exhibition space "nexus"

Floor plan "nexus"   scale 1:250
Section showcase   scale 1:10

a laminated glass 8 mm, visible edges polished
b steel profile ⊏⊐ 20/50 mm
c steel profile ⊏⊐ 20/50 mm, lateral perforation
d aluminum profile 20/20 mm, laterally connected LED
   modules, vertically adjustable
e glass panel, laminated glass 8 mm
f cable duct
g door frame, stainless steel, powder coated
h cladding, aluminum sheet metal, powder coated

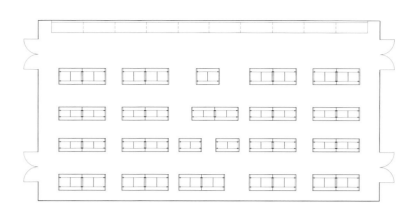

prets the building as house and the exhibition areas as spaces in a thoughtful way, and translates qualities of architecture into the exhibition. This results in the exhibition being neither illustrative nor narrative; it focuses on the sensual presence of materials, light, and shadow, and on simple forms. It treats the objects from the archive as physical items and also takes their visual quality into account.

The permanent exhibition disentangles the communication of literary texts and the presentation of archive inventory items by distributing them across two different spaces. And it differentiates between production and reception media in literature and what people leave behind in terms of documents, letters, photos, etc.

In "nexus", various, very different routes are possible. The exhibits are allocated to two main trajectories, literature and life, and laid out chronologically, according to the year in which they have, in the widest sense, been used by their originator or owner; in which they were e.g. created, bought, read, given away as present, rediscovered, left behind, in any case touched by someone. Visitors can stroll about, drift, simply watch, but also choose some select exhibits for a concentrated reading or just take a look at objects of an author, a time period, or with particular characteristics. The singular, "objectively correct" route does not exist. As working with literature shows: in aesthetic systems, consistent and coherent points of view and ways of reading exist side by side. They do not exclude each other, but contribute to each other.

Heike Gfrereis

3

Museum of Celtic and Roman History in Manching

Architects: Fischer Architekten, Munich

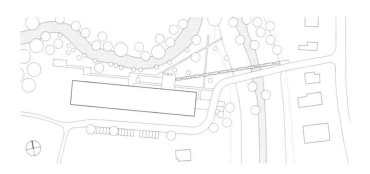

From a single source: In addition to the museum building, the architects also designed the interior architecture and showcases in the exhibition spaces.

The origins of the former Celtic town have been subject to scientific research beginning in the 19th century. Today, Manching is renowned across Europe for being the best researched historic Celtic settlement. After finding the remains of two 15 m long Roman ships about two kilometers away, an association was founded that worked towards keeping the historic finds in Manching. The state of Bavaria finally agreed to the concept for a new museum building on location. Designed as an oversize showcase, the 100 m long building, built on a limited budget, is located along a peninsula between the Augrabenbach stream and Paarkanal channel, bordering the Celtic wall of Manching. The upper level, mostly enclosed in translucent glass, features the exhibition area and rests upon a solid concrete base which houses depot and administration, as well as the glazed ship hall, visible from the museum park. At night, integrated fluorescent lighting illuminates the facade.

Maximum flexibility through open construction

The entrance on the upper level can be accessed by a gently rising 80 m long walkway, crossing the flood channel, which serves for receiving floodwater from the Augrabenbach. Upon entering the building, a temporal and spatial separation between visitors and the present time and place is intended to occur. The interior design concept immediately becomes obvious within the 400 m² area of the entrance hall: open

structural ceiling elements spanning the entire building width of 18 m create a column-free space with maximum flexibility. In order to meet acoustic demands, also in the lecture area, felt panels are suspended between ceiling members in the foyer. Admission, shop, and cafeteria are located in the entry foyer, and a temporary exhibition area in the shape of a black box is located to the left.

Permanent exhibition

To the right of the entrance hall, the roundtrip through the permanent exhibition begins in the largest space of the building, covering 800 m² and dedicated to the "Celts". Floor-to-ceiling glazing provides natural illumination through the northern facade. While maple wood gives the foyer a precious character, simple materials such as cement screed, reminiscent of natural stone, or sandblasted concrete walls dominate in the exhibition areas and create a restrained backdrop for the exhibits. Five suspended display cases and floor showcases comprise the backbone of the exhibition. Walking past the cube of the media space, visitors are led along connecting bridges into the "Roman" exhibition area. Visitors can view the almost 10 m tall ship hall from a gallery. Open staircases lead onto the ground level, where the facade opens to all sides to the exterior and visitors can take a closer look at the ships. A cabinet-like space, open to the hall, features further exhibits of Roman origin. Next to the rooms for museum education, visitors enter the covered open space in the exterior with its flowing transition into the neighboring museum park. Installations for individual experience and experimentation, e.g. an oven made of adobe are located here, intended to exemplify the living conditions of Celts and Romans in a playful way.

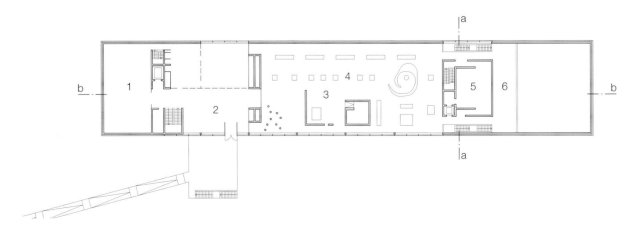

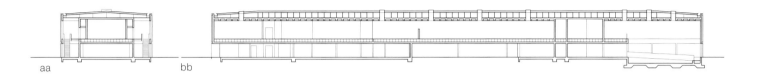

aa   bb

Site plan   scale 1:3,000
Sections • floor plans
scale 1:750

1 Temporary exhibition
2 Foyer
3 Permanent exhibition
   "Celts"
4 Floor display cases
5 Media space
6 Permanent exhibitions
   "Romans"
7 Museum education
   department
8 Depot
9 Administration

Project data:

Use:	cultural/education
Museum/collection type:	archaeological collection
Construction:	reinforced concrete
Clear room height:	3.6–4.2 m
Gross volume:	15,576 m³
Gross footprint:	3,074 m²
Exhibition area:	1,350 m²
Total cost:	€ 7.03 million
Completion:	2006
Construction time:	25 months

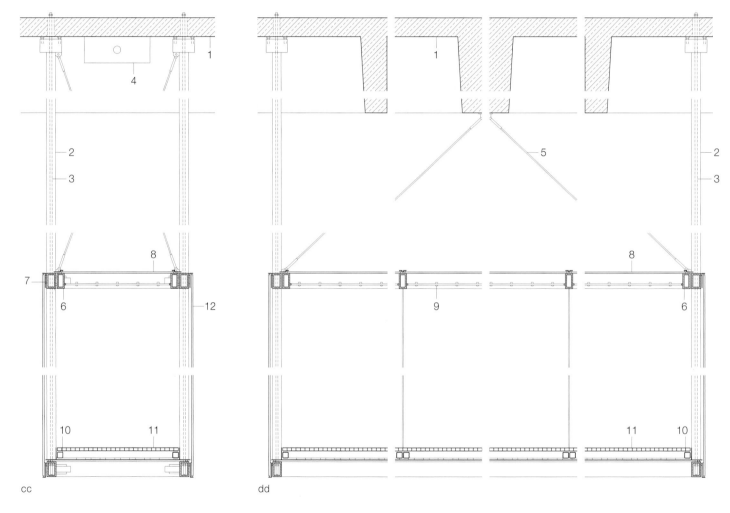

cc

dd

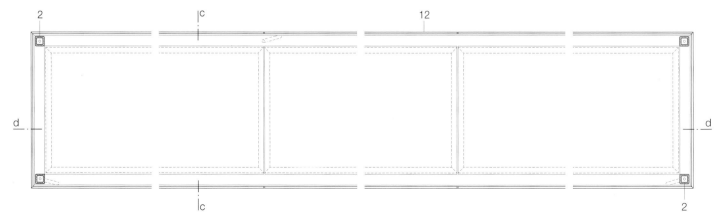

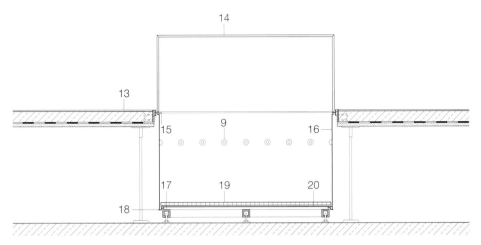

Vertical sections · horizontal section
suspended showcase
Vertical section floor showcase
scale 1:20

1 reinforced concrete ceiling/roof 100 mm
   beam depth 700 mm
2 suspended pipe, aluminum ⬚ 50/50/3
3 threaded rod ∅ 10 mm, ceiling-mount
4 lighting fixture 100 W
5 steel cable ∅ 6 mm
6 aluminum pipe ⬚ 80/40/3
7 framing, aluminum pipe ⬚ 80/50/5
8 upper casing, security glass panel 8 mm,
   matte adhesive foil
9 glass fiber lighting termination
10 aluminum pipe ⬚ 30/30/2
11 display panel, MDF transparent glaze finish
   16 mm, detachable in three components
12 showcase door, laminate glass 10 mm
13 raised cavity:
   hard aggregate top layer for heavy-duty use
   reinforced concrete floor 70 mm
   PE foil separation layer
   structural panel, gypsum based 18 mm
   cavity with supports 500 mm
   reinforced concrete ceiling 200–300 mm
14 showcase laminate glass 10 mm
15 aluminum profile T 30/30/2 mm
   flange 12 mm
16 sheet metal casing, all sides
17 framing, steel pipe ⬚ 40/40/3 mm
18 Z-profile, steel 16/25/25/3.5 mm
19 display panel, MDF tinted grey 16 mm
20 base panel, steel sheet metal 2 mm

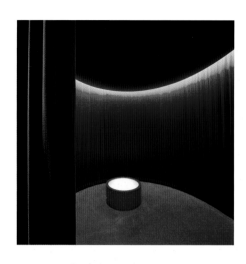

Vertical section · horizontal section
station "gold treasure"
scale 1:20

1 reinforced concrete ceiling 100 mm
  beam depth 700 mm
2 curtain, velour dark grey
3 wood trim, curved ⊡ 21/50 mm,
  drillings for mounting curtain hangers
4 aluminum grating, curved 80/40 mm
5 laminated veneer plywood sheathing 24/200 mm
6 LED indirect lighting
7 MDF cover panel with fabric covering
8 curtain, velour dark red
9 steel sheet metal door cladding 2 mm
10 display case, laminate glass, curved 10 mm
11 double floor, MDF grey imbued 16 mm
12 framing, steel profile, curved ⊡ 50/50/3 mm   ee

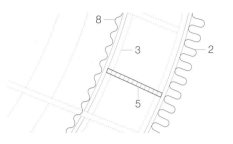

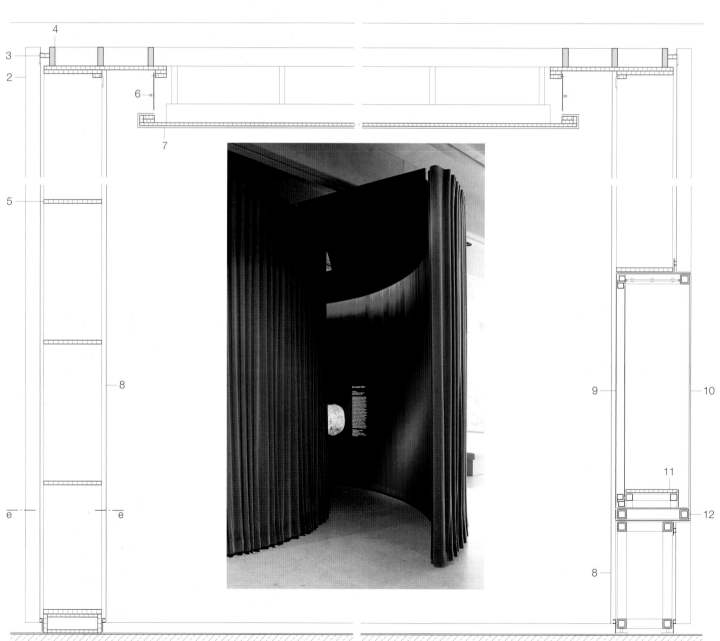

BMW Museum in Munich

Architects: ATELIER BRÜCKNER, Stuttgart
Media-based dramatizations: ART+COM, Berlin

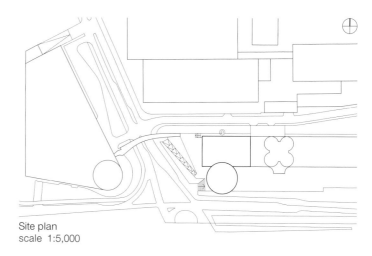

Site plan
scale 1:5,000

By expansion and redesign of a classic building, BMW opens new perspectives in the connection between architecture, exhibition design, and media.

Hardly any other building ensemble conveys the performance and philosophy of a corporation as effectively as the "four-cylinder" BMW administrative building and the bowl-shaped BMW museum. The "bowl" however, built more than thirty years ago by Viennese architect Karl Schwanzer, no longer meets the spatial demands of a contemporary exhibition concept. By incorporating the adjacent BMW low-rise administrative building, the available exhibition area was quintupled. This enabled creating an innovative museum concept. Guiding idea in Schwanzer's architectural design was the "continuation of the road in an enclosed space." Atelier Brückner adopted the idea and, based on it, developed a ramp system as central motif for architecture and exhibition.

Immersing in a fictitious city

Visitors begin their roundtrip in the new museum area housing the permanent exhibition. Along ramps leading below, they descend into a fictitious city. The facades of the 13 m tall exhibition houses consist of double satinized clear glazing backlit by more than 1.7 million LEDs. The oversized screens can project diverse images. Each of the seven houses has a motto and identity of its own, with a specific visual appearance as well as a corresponding exhibition design.

Specific appearances

The individual topic of an exhibition house pervades all "building" levels. The "House of Design" for instance deals with the design process of an automobile, from idea to design icon. Point of origin of the three-fold dramatization is the kinetic sculpture in the "inspiration"-space. The installation consists of 714 metal spheres that are suspended by delicate, flexible steel cables and can assume vehicle shapes typical for BMW by individual computer control. Beginning in a state akin to brainstorming, the choreography moves from associative ideas and geometrical shapes to the illustration of renowned vehicles.

The completely black treasure chamber in the "House of Design" presents design icons that have defined BMW's design until today. Rarities and one-offs are dramatized by directed illumination.

Other spaces are based on rather technical inspiration and equipment: a 30 m^2 media table presents itself as an interactive chronicle of the history of BMW. 90 years of company history are documented by means of texts, pictures and films, which provide information on vehicles and motors. The table can be operated via a multitouch surface sensitive to the touch.

Content first, then technology

Despite all multimedia innovation, technology is mostly concealed. The goal is to have visitors interact with the displayed content. All elements can be operated intuitively and react to the presence of visitors. The BMW museum becomes a sensual and surprising experience, rich in its communicated content.

Project data:

Use:	cultural/education
Museum/collection type:	brand/automotive museum
Construction:	reinforced concrete
Clear height:	13 m
Gross volume:	70,585 m^2
Gross footprint:	12,200 m^2
Exhibition area:	5,000 m^2
Total cost:	€ 80 million (gross)
Completion:	2008
Construction time:	20 months

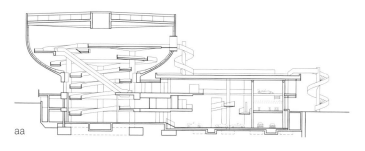

aa

a|

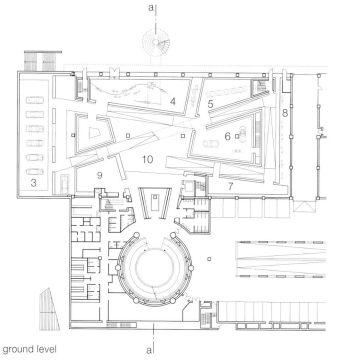

4 5 8
6
10
9
3 7

ground level   a|

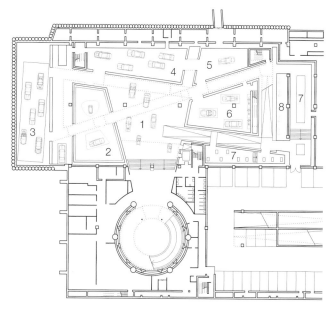

4 5
7
1 6 8
3
2 7

sublevel

Floor plans · section
scale 1:1,000

1 BMW Plaza
2 "House of the Brand"
3 "House of the Series"
4 "House of Motor Sport"
5 "House of Technology"
6 "House of Design"

7 "House of the Company"
8 "House of the Motorcycle"
9 Seminar space
10 Void BMW plaza
11 Cafeteria
12 Museum shop
13 Foyer
14 Special exhibition area
   in the "bowl"

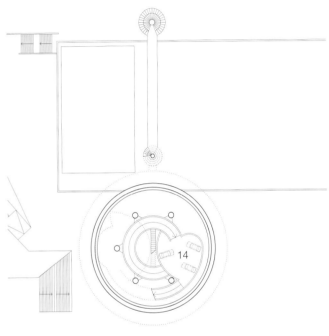

level 2

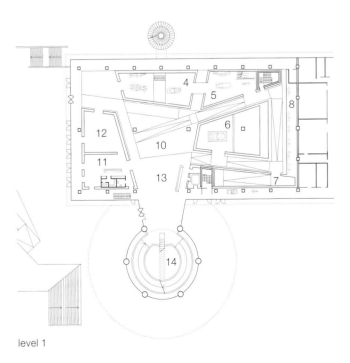

level 1

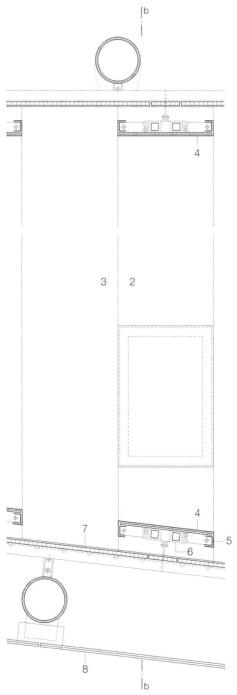

Horizontal section · vertical section
"Aspects" exhibition space
"House of the Company"
scale 1:20

1 composite floor 100 mm
2 flooring, aluminum sheet metal,
   anodized 3/520 mm
   wood composite material 19 mm,
   adhered to leveling layer
3 flooring, clear laminate glass 2× 6 mm
   satinized, adhered to leveling layer
4 aluminum sheet metal, anodized,
   canted edge 3 mm
5 aluminum profile ⌴ 60/60/60 mm
6 fluorescent strip lighting

7 facing, clear security glass 4 mm, satinized
   composite wood material panel 19 mm
   LED lighting
   fixture, aluminum profile ⌴ 35/35/3 mm
   strut, steel hollow profile ⊡ 40/60 mm
   column, steel pipe ⌀ 244 mm
8 laminate prestressed glass 2× 10 mm
   glass fitting, polished stainless steel
9 aluminum sheet metal, canted edge 3 mm
   MDF 19 mm
   framing, aluminum profile ⌴ 60/60/4 mm
   aluminum sheet metal, canted edge
   magnetic fixture
10 aluminum hollow profile ⊡ 60/60/4 mm
11 downlight

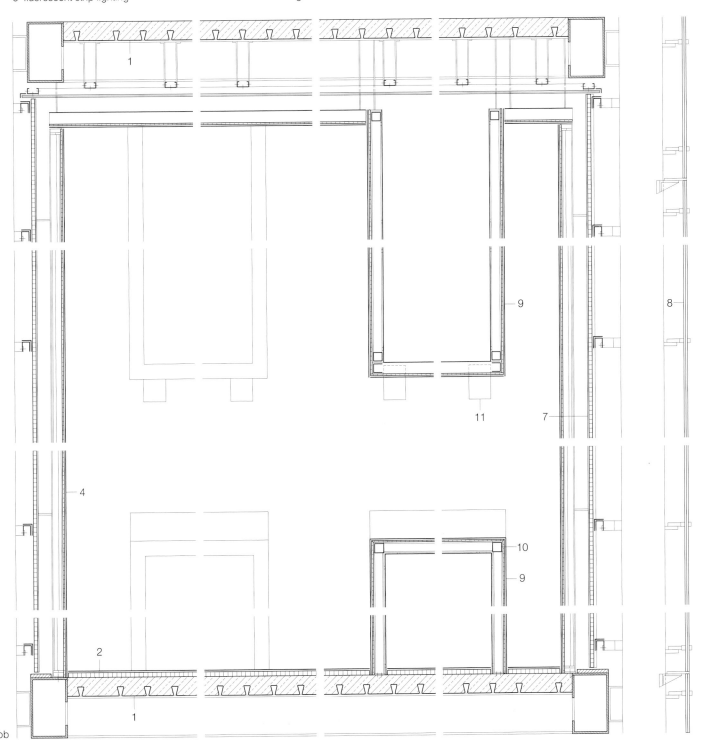

bb

47

Elevation · vertical section
Display sphere in the "bowl"
scale 1:20

1 display sphere ⌀ 800 mm
  white finish perspex 10 mm
2 glass cover, clear security glass 6 mm
  graphic text layer
3 acrylic glass, light dispersive 6 mm
  graphic layer image
4 fluorescent lighting ring
5 steel mount 8 mm adhered to sphere segment
6 steel pipe ⌀ 159 mm
7 parapet, reinforced concrete 20 mm
8 floor construction:
  poured asphalt, sanded 50 mm
  separating layer
  reinforced concrete 250 mm

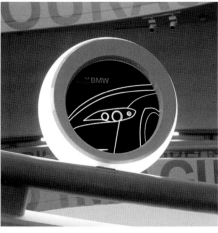

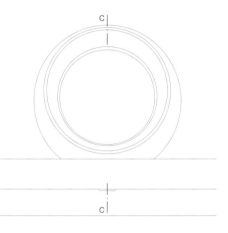

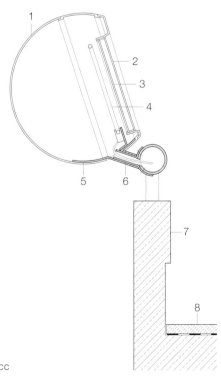

1

Conceptualizing a brand museum
Dramatizing the brand – museum concept and exhibition design

The term corporate architecture is currently the talk of the town. Architecture has the capacity to mobilize, lure people into remote corners of the world, and simultaneously express the brand message of a corporation. In hindsight, the most convincing buildings are those conceptually originated within corporate identity. In this context, corporate scenography becomes increasingly significant, transforming corporate identity into spatial images and enabling an authentic brand experience via choreographed spatial dramatizations. By integration and adequate dosage of all relevant design methods, scenography has the capability to generate brand experiences with reminder value. With the BMW museum as an example, this will be illustrated in the following.

A museum offers the unique opportunity of turning an abstract brand idea into a real-time experience, connecting it with its history, and at the same time indicating its future potential. It thus includes a lot more than only displaying the expansive collections of a corporation. The goal is to dramatize the brand within the context of a museum.

Ramp system

For the completely gutted interior of the low-rise building adjacent to the so-called museum "bowl", Atelier Brückner designed an impressively structured spatial landscape intended to convey momentum and innovation. The guiding idea for the museum bowl, the continuation of the street into enclosed space, defined in the 1970s by Karl Schwanzer, was re-adapted, re-thought, and re-interpreted. Central motif for architecture and exhibition was the ramp system, seemingly floating freely through the space. As a defined and defining element, it assumes a key position. It leads visitors through the museum and connects the new permanent exhibition with the "bowl".

Along the ramp system, visitors delve into the BMW city. They proceed along the polished asphalt surface as if walking on a street providing access to the individual, topically defined exhibition houses.

Exhibition houses

The brand color white is the defining element for this permanent exhibition. The houses appear as homogeneous, gleaming structures with bright shining glass facades. The exhibition spaces as such are designed as "white cubes". The

spaces are differentiated by defining an individual topic for each house: design, motorcycles, technology, motor sport, series, company, and brand. The identity of the houses is visible on all stories. Joint design elements are comprehensively employed on all levels and exemplify the vertical, topical structuring of all exhibition areas.

Visitors enter the houses from the street. Large door openings offer views of the interior and raise curiosity for exhibits and their dramatization. Visual axes emphasize the content-based interconnections both inside a house as well as between houses. Thus e.g. in the "House of Design", the design process from the initial idea to its implementation can be experienced spatially. The glass floor enables a view – backward and forward – into the other levels of the house (ill. 4).

The original, authentic object is always in the center of the exhibition and is point of origin for each spatial dramatization. It provides a foundation for the differentiation of individual exhibition areas. Placed in the center of a space, it unfolds its aura without inhibition. Based on a comprehensive design gesture for each exhibition house, each object or object group is dramatized according to the related subject. Thus, spatial images are developed that are generated from the specific content.

"House of the Company"

Within the "House of the Company" for instance, different aspects of corporate history are introduced to the visitor. The room "First Steps. How everything began" shows the history of the Bavarian Motor Works from its beginnings in airplane engine production in 1917 ("Beginnings high up in the air") to the construction of the first motorcycle in 1927 ("Success on two wheels") to the purchase of the vehicle factory in Eisenach in 1928 and BMW's resulting step into automotive manufacturing ("First steps on four wheels"). The exhibits are integrated into a "temporal space" made of sculpturally designed white and silver colored frames. In particular locations, they open up and create temporal windows in which exhibits are presented in the context of their particular era.

The other rooms in the house are also designed as temporal windows. As the name indicates, the room "Aspects. Thought and Action" located below provides insight into aspects of corporate history. Subjects include global networking, built communication, individual responsibility, enthusiasm, customer orientation, trust, quality, and flexibility, yet also forced

labor in the Third Reich. Large format date numbers organize the topics in relation to corporate history. A picture book is dedicated to each of these subjects. Placed on eight consoles, they invite visitors to have a look. By use of a tracking system, matching audio text is played along with the pictorial content and informs visitors via directed loudspeakers. In addition, visitors receive a comprehensive overview of the 90-year history and all BMW products in the "Chronology" room. The dimmed illumination creates a mystical atmosphere. Delicate cello sounds support the magic of the dramatization. The central exhibit is an interactive media table measuring 30 m², the so-called corporate sculpture. It has multitouch capacity, i.e. multiple visitors can simultaneously access different information by touching the table surface and can thus immerse themselves into the history of BMW.

The media-based dramatization was developed individually for each room by the Berlin-based design office Art+Com. Media-based choreography consisting of projections, light, and sound enhance the cmessage of each room. Interactive installations and so-called serving formats such as e.g. info-bars provide visitors with additional, in-depth information. Visitors are actively included into the exhibition event. Technical aspects recede into the background. The installations are not intrusive, but are an integrated component of architecture and overall dramatization.

BMW Plaza

The apex of the media-based dramatization is, without a doubt, the BMW Plaza (ill. 1). It is the beating heart in the center of the permanent exhibition; the exhibition houses encircle it. Visitors repeatedly encounter this 13 m tall void on their roundtrip. Its dramatization enables mobilization of space and recipient. The facades of the exhibition houses, covering approximately 700 m², include LED technology generating either abstract or topical imagery. They feature more than 1.7 million lighting diodes. 30 possible settings create an environment of digital imagery that facilitates an atmosphere of technological, but at the same time poetic-emotional dimensions. The architecture becomes dematerialized and dynamic. In connection with a video tracking system, this so-called mediatecture can also be switched into reactive mode. The media imagery thus reacts to the presence of visitors and integrates them actively into the scenario. Based on extensive testing, parameters were determined that create an impressive, coherent spatial experience, corresponding to the brand, by connecting architecture and media technology. The implemented concept employs monochrome white LEDs fixed behind double satinized clear glazing. The glazing contributes to a unified, coherent appearance and concealment of technology from the view of the visitor – even from up close. They do not perceive the glass panes as a construction component placed in front of the LEDs; instead, the houses seem to glow from within.

Altogether, a gracious, spacious overall impression is created. The "visual transparency" of construction components, generally comprised of glass or polished stainless steel, supports this impression. Even the central bridge, along which visitors cross the BMW plaza, is inobstrusive in its appearance. Together with Schlaich Bergermann und Partner, the Stuttgart-based architects developed an innovative glass bridge construction that uses structural glass as side walls.

For the tension members of the bridge, special steel cabling until now only used for racing yachts was selected; it is thinner than usual while simultaneously possessing stronger tensile capacity. As result, the envisioned design goals led to future-oriented innovations in architectural detailing.

Visual symphony

The BMW Plaza can be interpreted as prologue of the museum, since it comprises the first space that visitors consciously perceive. With its media imagery, it can be read as an oversize "table of contents" of the entire museum. The epilogue of the museum unfolds itself on the topmost platform of the museum bowl. Via the BMW Plaza, visitors can access the bowl. The exhibition design emphasizes the architectural quality of this spectacular space, with its prior interior design now removed and architecturally connected to the addition for the opening of the new museum. Spheres made of translucent plastic, attached to handrails, provide a rhythmic structure. They feature text and graphics of exhibited vehicles and their historic context.

Visitors are drawn up the ramp as if attracted by a vortex, comprised of the so-called "visual symphony" on the topmost platform of the bowl. Impressions perceived along the approximately one kilometer long roundtrip are triggered anew and are atmospherically charged. The extraordinary column-free space with a diameter of 40 m and a height of up to 6 m permits a 360° panorama projection along the interior wall of the building facade (director: Marc Tamschick, Berlin).

Through media imagery, the space unfolds itself. A holistic experience of space, image, and sound takes visitors on a journey into the great, dynamic world of the Bavarian Motor Works. 18 projections are connected into a moving surround-image. 125 loudspeakers and 64 audio channels are placed similar to musicians in an orchestra. Produced in real-time, the media presentation is of indefinite length. The basis for this is an audiovisual sound landscape; its fragments are subtly reminiscent of prior dramatizations. At regular intervals, the media presentation changes, and thus an impressive spatial sound experience is created as conclusion and apex of the museum roundtrip.

Epilogue

Within its corporate headquarters, BMW created a truly "automotive museum", in which architecture, content message, and design interact. Based on BMW's brand philosophy and the local historic situation, new solutions in design were envisioned and implemented. The original museum concept, "the street in an enclosed space", received a contemporary new interpretation, i.e. "the street within enclosed space as principle of dynamic architecture" (Uwe R. Brückner). Here, the proverbial "Sheer Driving Pleasure" becomes a spatial event and enables visitors to perceive the brand BMW as a real, authentic experience in space. Thus, a mobile and motivating museum architecture – corporate scenography – was created for the BMW corporation.

Eberhard Schlag, Claudia Luxbacher

1 BMW Plaza
2 Ramp and walkway system, view towards "House of the Series"
3 "Advertisement" space, timeline, "House of the Brand"
4 "Inspiration" space, kinetic sculpture, "House of Design"
5 Ramp and walkway system, view towards BMW Plaza

5

Mercedes-Benz Museum in Stuttgart

Architects: UNStudio, Amsterdam
Exhibition design: hg merz, Stuttgart

Project data:

Use:	cultural/education
Museum/exhibition type:	brand/automotive museum
Construction:	reinforced concrete
Gross volume:	270,000 m³
Gross footprint:	25,000 m²
Exhibition area:	16,500 m²
Total construction cost:	€ 150 million (gross)
Completion:	2006
Construction time:	33 months

Interwined spaces, created by the double-helix structure, facilitate switching from one exibition vector to another.

Located next to the parent plant in Stuttgart-Untertürkheim, Mercedes-Benz created a monument, visible from afar, symbolizing the brand, its history, and most of all the automobiles. When racing along the four-lane highway, this sculptural building, characterized by a metallic sheen and glass strips at varying degrees of inclination, at first appears as a mystery. The exterior skin however reflects a unique interior organization.

Interior organization
The museum entrance is lifted up from the ground surface by one story in order to elevate the museum function from its industrial surrounding. Elevators accompanied by audiovisual media transport visitors from the atrium onto the topmost level. The roundtrip through the building begins here.
The spatial organization of the building resembles a double helix. The symmetry of the clover-like floor plan is further transformed by individual rotation of floors, thus creating the vertical alignment of spaces. The clover leaves circle around a triangular atrium and comprise five horizontal levels, each consisting of a one or two story element (for the Collections or the Myth Scenes).
The five two-story Myth Spaces, oriented towards the atrium, feature highlights of corporate history in chronological succession – the "Mercedes Myth". The five so-called "Collections",

single story spaces oriented towards the exterior, receive a topical imagery and, due to natural illumination, contrast the dramatized Myth Spaces. Cross linkages on each level permit visitors to create an individual route through both units. The roundtrip terminates spectacularly in the exhibition unit "Silver Arrows", depicting the brand's history in automotive sports.

Structure
This architectural experiment – considered stacked bridges from the point of view of structural engineering, skyscraper and assembly building according to fireproofing standards, and terra incognita for many project partners – needed to be completed in a relatively short amount of time, before begin of the Soccer World Championships in 2006. The structure resembling a double helix produces an absence of straight walls, with the exception of the interior face of the elevator shafts. Most walls are curved not only along one axis, but are doubly curved, similar to propeller blades or marine screw propellers. Thus, the necessary software and the majority of plans were created while construction was already under way. In this process, all planning steps were 3D computer based and integrated into a centrally managed data model, the so-called mother model, as geometric reference. Construction of this sculptural design was only possible with cast-in-place concrete. In this regard, the creation of even surfaces for anticlastic building components was a special challenge. Every piece of concrete formwork was unique, created by computer-controlled milling machines.

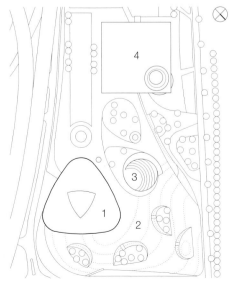

Site plan
scale 1:4,000

1 Mercedes-Benz Museum
2 Plaza
3 Open air arena
4 Mercedes-Benz Center

level 0

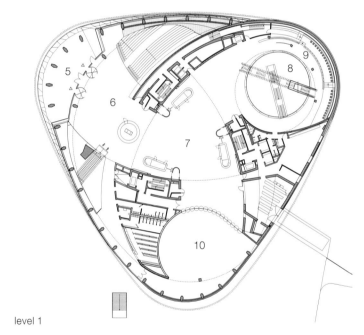

level 1

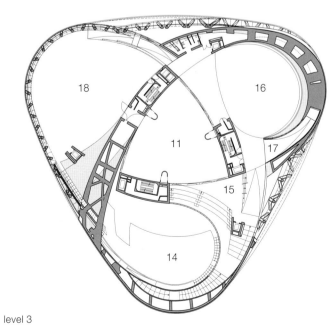

level 3

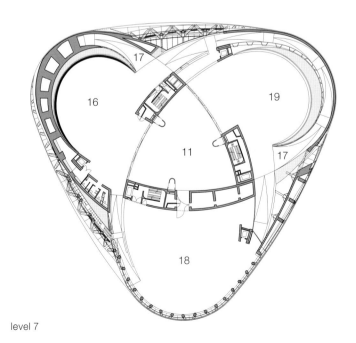

level 7

Floor plan
scale 1:1,000

1 Exhibition "Fascination of Technology"
2 Utilities
3 Storage
4 Walkway to Mercedes-Benz Center
5 Main entrance
6 Foyer
7 Atrium
8 Void "Fascination of Technology"
9 Cafeteria
10 Auditorium
11 Void atrium
12 Banked track "Silver Arrows" (Myth 7)
13 Administration
14 Banked track
15 Grandstand
16 Myth level
17 Ramp between Myth levels/ Illustrated Timeline
18 Collections level
19 Void Myth
20 Arrival platform
21 Exhibition starting point (Myth 1)
22 Event level
23 Roof terrace

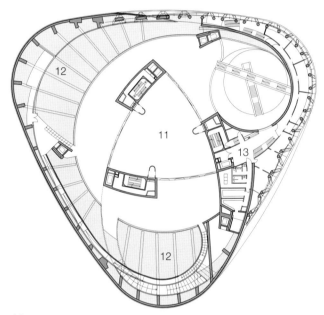

level 2

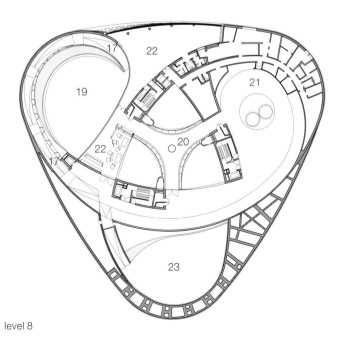

level 8

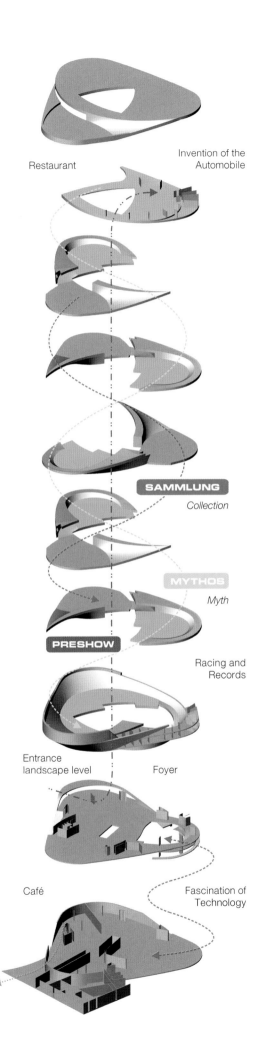

Restaurant

Invention of the Automobile

SAMMLUNG
Collection

MYTHOS
Myth

PRESHOW

Racing and Records

Entrance landscape level

Foyer

Café

Fascination of Technology

55

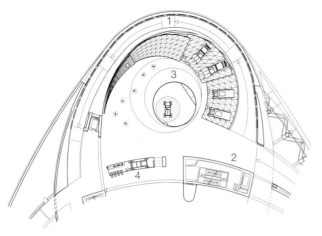

Floor plan Myth 2
"Birth of the Brand"
1 Illustrated Timeline
2 Core Wall
3 Scene
4 Workbench

The approximately 80 m long "Illustrated Timeline" is adapted to the curvature of the facade. Its supporting construction consists of steel consoles, which serve as fixtures for aluminum frames suspended between them. These carry the facing for 27 image and object showcases (exchangeable if required) and provide connection points for them. The recessed casing includes all technical components such as projectors, fiberglass lighting, lighting frames, and fluorescent strip lighting. These together create a homogeneous lighting mood. Since these can only be maintained from the front, the visible showcase frame (fixed by six bolts placed in a recess gap) is removable.

The photographs placed in the image showcases are rastered and printed onto two glass panes placed back to back.

Light raster dots are on the front, darker raster dots are on the back pane, thus creating an impression of depth. A third pane featuring lettering is placed in front of this arrangement. A lighting frame is mount behind the panes. It consists of two fluorescent strip lights, hidden beneath the upper and lower showcase cover, and a acrylic glass diffusion panel with white raster dot print for reflecting light. The number of raster dots controls light intensity and thus serves for adapting to different lighting situations. The object showcases include only a front glass pane for lettering. Their back panel is illuminated and serves for mounting the exhibits. Behind each object, a part of the back panel surface is painted grey to prevent glare. Fiberglass spotlights in the upper showcase cover direct light onto exhibits. Additionally, a fluorescent strip light provides homogeneous lighting in the entire showcase.

Illustrated timeline
(here: Myth 5 "Safety and the Environment")
Vertical sections • horizontal sections
scale 1:10
A Image showcase
B Object showcase

5   airbag fabric surface material
    styrofoam B1 5 mm
    plywood panel 13 mm
    MDF strip 19 mm
6   framing
    aluminum profile 60/40 mm
7   recessed casing, steel sheet metal 3 mm
    elongated bolt holes
8   aluminum profile 15/15/3 mm for bolt
    connection between showcase and
    recessed casing
9   showcase frame, anodized aluminum
10 polycarbonate, clear 6 mm,
    with printed lettering
11 float glass 5 mm, silkscreen print
12 acrylic glass, matte printed 6/10 mm
13 sighting frame system: diffusion panel,
    acrylic glass, matte printed 10 mm,
    backlit above/below
14 MDF trim
    gap white semi-gloss
15 painted sheet metal facing 3 mm
16 projector
17 fiberglass spotlight, adjustable
18 diffusion panel,
    translucent acrylic glass 6 mm
19 fluorescent light strip

A

aa   bb   B

Workbench
Top view   scale 1:100
Vertical sections   scale 1:20

1 recess for touch element
2 showcase
3 media station
4 showcase drawer
5 monitor, video exhibit
   (removable for maintenance)
6 microcinema
7 plastic ceramic surface
8 framing, wood composite material
9 cross flow fan

10 monitor casing
    (removable for maintenance)
11 ventilation feed-through
12 steel pipe ▱ 60/30 (monitor suspension)
13 loudspeakers
14 perforated stainless steel sheet metal,
    glass pearl finish, painted white
15 security glass, anti-reflective coating 10 mm
    (disassembly for maintenance)
16 fiberglass spotlight, adjustable
17 diffusion panel, acrylic glass 10 mm
18 panel (removable for maintenance)
19 fluorescent strip light
    (removable for maintenance)

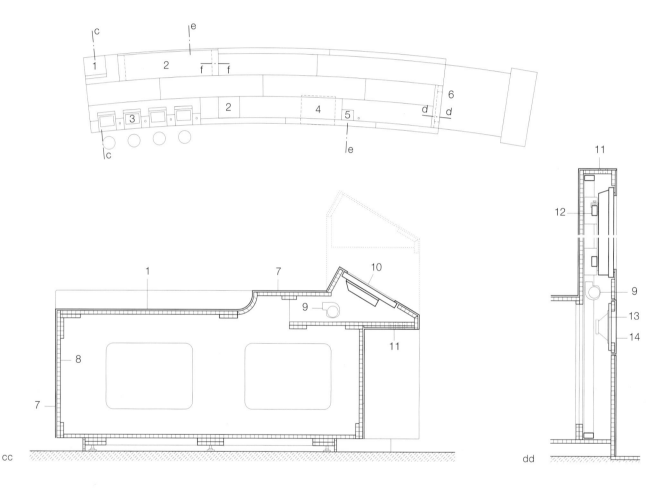

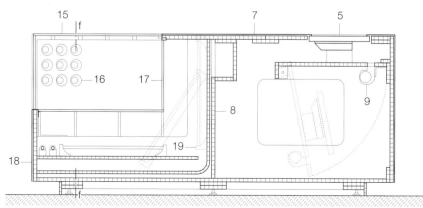

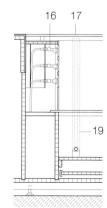

The Workbenches are comprised of tables spanning eleven meters in length. Their focus is to convey technical and design-oriented innovations of high significance. Topics such as compressor and diesel technology or the development of ABS and airbag are paid tribute to in detail with exhibits, texts, graphics, and films. The Workbench casing is comprised of up to 40 components. However, their surfaces appear seamless, yet are visually divided by a designed placement of grooves relating to exhibits and featured illustrations. The plastic ceramic used here enables seamless and invisible corner and butt joints. The mineral-based composite material is mixed with a fireproof wood-based aggregate and form-pressed. Highest degrees of precision and cleanliness are necessary in treating joints in order to achieve a homogeneous overall impression. The framing of Workbenches is comparable to cross wall construction for shipbuilding. Cross-ties made of wood composite material serve as stiffeners. In places where Workbenches support heavy objects, a steel frame transmits loads into the floors.

Global expansion is on the center stage of Myth 6 "Global and Individual" (illustration below). Five vehicles with high mileage display the brand's international and individual character. The media ring hovers above this setting: including 48 monitors, with 19.5 m diameter, weighing 11.6 tons, it comprises the most impressive built component of the museum interior. The ring was assembled from 48 components on-site and "jacked up" by four scaffolds in order to install it in its final position below the ceiling. A mesh tube construction supports the monitors, oriented towards the interior, and the LED-band specifically designed for this construction (LED pads placed behind a diffuser disc), running along the exterior surface of the ring. It consists of rectangular steel profiles assembled into a curved box girder. The surface of the media ring consists of precast elements made of fiberglass-reinforced plastic with high gloss paint finish. For creating video content, the responsible team traveled more than 100,000 kilometers by plane. When visitors watch the installation for a couple of minutes, they can experience the sun's movement across the globe.

Show and let show

HG Merz, Patrick Wais

The second life of things –
What it means to design exhibitions

A current production of the "Meistersinger von Nürnberg" at the Nationaltheater in Mannheim begins with chorus and protagonists in an austerely designed exhibition space with suspended, tiled ceiling, grey walls, and obligatory parquet floor. Jens-Daniel Herzog's production transforms the Katharinenkirche in Nuremberg into a typical museum space – in a certain way also a sacred space – an "aesthetic national church."[1] The audience worships the sanctified exhibit: a Meistersinger outfit, placed in a showcase just as all other important Meistersinger props, such as singing chairs and Beckmesser's lute. Finally, at the climax of glorifying "holy German art", the assumed renovator Walther von Stolzing and his Eva vanish behind panes of glass. Only Hans Sachs, stepping forward from a scene that freezes into a static image, is capable of liberating himself from this "total conservation". Pointing to the stage as if it were a painting, he is artist and museum guide in one.

The production plays with the subject of conservation on multiple levels. However, only its relevance in regard to design and scenography of exhibitions is of interest to us. Richard Wagner's Meistersinger resemble historic material in two ways: both the historic setting of the musical-dramatical plot, as well as "art-as-religion" originating in the spirit of music, seem to belong to the past. Figures and props have long since assumed their position within the showcases of a "musée imaginaire" of art and cultural history, oscillating between amnesia and adoration. On stage, trying to materialize the past in the present is met with failure. As modernists, we are detached from our own history, whether we like it or not. The second life of physical relics is limited to the protective space of the museum. Re-socialization and re-integration into the world of the living is bound to fail.

Dealing with the difference between an object in a museum, i.e. the exhibit, and life beyond the museum is part of our day-to-day business as exhibition designers. This difference plays a significant role for the ongoing discourse. Conservationism has been subject to criticism for some time, and the contrast between lifelessness on the one hand and vividness on the other is the basis of the critique of conservation. Boris Groys for instance accuses museum makers of "vampiristic practices"[2] as museums profit from the death of things and of life on a general basis. Philipp Blom doesn't stop here. In a

piece for ZEIT titled "Get rid of museums!", he offers a diagnosis of the profound interest in dead material as exhibited by a culture that lacks "courage for ephemereality" and in which "...one cannot walk one step without stepping on the toes of a curator."[3] At present it seems obvious that the schism between yesterday and today, the "rift in time"[4], is becoming bigger and bigger than ever before within a "velociferous"[5] society of devilish acceleration. The moment you just experienced becomes history just a moment later. This is why Stolzing is transformed into an exhibit immediately after becoming a Meistersinger, following his revolutionary innovation.

Given that such critical interventions are correct at least in part, we see our task precisely in bringing these contrasts back together through the means of exhibition design available to us. Even though it may sound exalted, this implies transforming forgotten or suppressed history into tradition, into personal and acquired history, in order to bridge the chasm between yesterday and today as far as possible. The way we see it, questions of practice and function of a museum become questions on how to put something on display: What kind of exhibits and design methods do we use for showing history? How, spoken with the words of Gottfried Korff, do we provide museum objects with an "expository resurrection?" By asking these questions, we touch upon the core of the museum itself, as we experience the exhibits and narratives that are presented in a museum in a particular contextual mode. In other words: We never perceive exhibits simply the way they are, but by the way they are presented to us. As result, exhibition designers are expected to design and compose spatial arrangements that visualize history and convey a certain message. In our opinion, this process of visualization is directed by the dictum of modesty and tact. We do not impose a form upon the narratives and objects, but instead aid them in displaying themselves according to their particular characteristics and personality.

In other words: we set the stage for these things. We conceptually and architecturally design spaces and situations in which the exhibits can present themselves and tell their stories, thus providing them with a second life. We create configurations, one may also say productions, which are comprised of objects, text, media, and atmospheres, and create an exhibition by determining their sequence and order. In this regard, the "stage handicraft" of the exhibition designer has logic, rules, and requirements of its own, even though we as well are interested in displaying protagonists, interrelations, and developments. Thus, scenography means to formally and dramaturgically design exhibition spaces so visitors have access to and can experience worlds past and distant, known and unknown.

Hands and minds – what exhibition design means

The same rules apply to Hans Sachs, both cobbler and Meistersinger, as well as to the exhibition designer: Their activity is both mental and manual. Working on ideas and forms goes hand in glove. Both provide a corrective for each other: The technical possibilities for thought and concept; the exhibition topics and goals for the craft of architecture. In abstract and formulaic terms, the designer's activity can be described as follows: We produce spaces in order to conduce the exhibits on display so they may introduce themselves in a manner appropriate to them. Three key aspects determine the work of exhibition designers dealing with this kind of synergy: concept follows content, exhibition architecture, and visual communication. The exhibit represents the essence of these aspects. It constitutes the most important component of each exhibition, as museums and exhibitions exclusively legitimize themselves through the presentation of objects and their aesthetic and narrative qualities. In cases in which the exhibit receives only a subordinate, illustrative meaning, the exhibition becomes redundant and can be replaced by illustrated volumes, text, or film. This is why scenographic conceptions are originated in the network of interrelations of exhibit, architecture, lighting, material, and media. The resulting manifold interactions stimulate, delimit, and modify each other. Thus it is often impossible to retrace afterwards who or what triggered which concept and implementation: "Exhibition planning is not an additive, but a simultaneously networked dialectical process that develops from a dialog between verbal-conceptual and visual-concrete rhetoric."[6]

We develop a superordinate dramaturgy and scenographic ideas based on exhibition concepts, floor plans, diagrams, and lists of selected and potential exhibits. However, one has to be careful when dealing with the topics of dramaturgy and scenography. The translation from the world of the stage to exhibition design is only possible to a limited degree, as the spatial situation in a museum is principally different from the auditorium in the theater or the opera. Whereas latter is characterized by a static and frontal juxtaposition of production and viewer, the museum has to be prepared for visitors who move freely on the stage and often undermine dramaturgic and scenographic endeavors by their patterns of movement.

Despite or just because the exhibition designer needs to be prepared for the subversive potential of the visitor, scenography and dramaturgy are of decisive importance. The great story arc, the central idea that leads the visitor through the exhibition, features a clear structure, and this structure is reflected in spatial dramatizations; dramatizations that are not only oriented frontally but can be observed from all sides. The great narrative keeps the many little tales, episodes, and events together and gives them a sensible and plausible place. This structure is not necessarily identical with a chronology of events. Other and better patterns of organization

than time or history are often more appropriate: typologies, genealogies, topics, and more. Whether it makes more sense to choose the one alternative or the other, combine them, or do something completely different, often becomes apparent only during the course of the project. Ideally, working with these stories and collections of exhibits allows us to develop methods of how to sort, how to juxtapose, and how to display them. In this regard, it is important to note that a clear narrative structure does not imply an uncritical presentation. The stories open a field of opportunities that also provides space for the ambivalent, the questionable, and the irrational, next to clear-cut questions. By now it is a well known fact in museum research that conservationist modes of presentation are less affirmative than critical, that they give preference to the foreign and the alien as opposed to simple repetition and affirmation of what people have already seen and already know.

We realize that the exhibition designer is indeed related to the set designer, even though he mainly deals with objects rather than humans. A stage set basically meets three functions: spatially and temporally define a scene or event, allocate positions for the protagonists' actions, as well as physically enable or support these actions via furniture or props. A set designer asks himself the following question: which kind of space do my protagonists need? As we all know, the answers can be extremely varied, in a museum and on the theater stage as well.
A look at the history of the museum shows that proposed solutions oscillate between two poles that each represent a completely different way of dealing with an exhibit. The Egyptian courtyard in the Neues Museum Berlin by Friedrich August Stüler is a prime example for what we call mimetic space. The courtyard represents a space that is mimetically adapted to the exhibit. Architecture, illustration, and ornament create an illusion of an Egyptian temple and thus almost completely erase the difference between presentation and exhibit, between original and copy. The monumental sculptures almost fully blend in with their environment; their visual presence indicates no significant difference between object and space. This is proof of a trust in the power of illusion that seems alien to us today.

The "white cube", the neutral space, comprises the antithesis to mimetic space. Within this space, every element of mimesis or contextual adaptation to the exhibit has vanished. It separates objects from the exterior world. As exhibition space, it is solely a backdrop from which everything stands out. It refrains from making any statement, even if only seemingly so. Seemingly, as the complete absence of the mimetic aspect clearly reflects the rejection of the illusionary in all its possible manifestations. The attention is focused and concentrated on one or multiple similarly denuded exhibits so that the entire power of explication is bound between object and observer. As opposed to Stüler's Egyptian courtyard, the "white cube" creates the greatest conceivable difference between presentation and presented object.

The neutral space for presentation of works of art still seems to be the state-of-the-art, whereas mimetic space has fallen from grace among most, however not all exhibition designers. To this day, these two types of space, each expressing a particular attitude towards the relation of space and object, are the poles and ideals that define the work of the set designer. In addition, both ideals represent different manifestations of sensual phenomena that provide an exhibition space with a particular mood and atmosphere. In general, three different tools are available to the exhibition designer: light, color, and material. The way in which these are used and how their relationship is articulated results in the creation of individual spaces. The exhibition designer acknowledges and makes use of the fact that spaces contain atmospheric qualities. These can be attractive or repulsive to visitors; can be considered pleasant or adverse. The exhibition designer also takes into account that the museum visitor experiences an exhibition with his physical body and all his senses. This is why we consider conservationist synaesthesia of perceived sensations as the normal case of a museum visit: It simultaneously comprises, in almost any moment, seeing, moving, and listening, often also feeling and smelling. Various test phases are often required until the right composition has been found, the search for the right material, the matching colors and the perfect spotlights and ambient lighting. This testing however is absolutely necessary in order to create coherent and attractive exhibition spaces, in which every detail contributes to the success of an appropriate encounter between visitors, exhibits, and the exhibition topics.

So much for a short, general summary of what it means to create concepts and designs for exhibitions, develop dramaturgy, and dramatize space. As we all know, in reality things usually don't develop the way we envision them on paper, detached from practice. The discrepancy between theory and practice is one aspect. The more important one is however the difference between the topic and the narratives that different exhibitions display. There is a difference between designing a brand museum for an automotive manufacturer or an exhibition on the site of a former concentration camp. A difference not only in regard to choice of exhibits and written content, but one that deeply forms our modus operandi and significantly characterizes our design endeavors.

Between worlds –
Why two exhibitions are never the same
As exhibition designers, we consider ourselves literally "between worlds" due to the heterogeneous nature of the range of tasks we deal with. The following features three examples as basis for discussing this range. These examples are what we describe as visual depot, modern chamber of wonders, and epic museum.

We understand a visual depot as an exhibition that employs a minimal design vocabulary in order to emphasize singular objects as such, undisturbed by architectural or graphic playfulness, and without excessive didactics. Examples for this are the Porsche Museum and the Glass Collection of the State Museum of Württemberg, both in Stuttgart, but as a special case also the "Station Z" on the grounds of the former concentration camp Sachsenhausen. The modern chamber of wonders however is seen as a form of presentation that displays a very heterogeneous collection of objects and lore, however it distances itself from excessive order and taxonomy. Sometimes there is a complex interrelation of exhibits

2

3

4

5

that evade singular classification, as they were integrated into completely different times, cultures, and practices. This is appropriately expressed by situation and contextualization within the new chamber of wonders. The epic museum finally may comprise elements of both, i.e. it offers the opportunity for concentration on the singular object as well as insight into the multilayered texture of narratives and events. Beyond that however, and this is the major difference, the epic museum represents a hermetic totality, a large superordinate narrative that allocates all aspects of the exhibition in a sensible way. Each of these three types thus represents a special kind of presentation, comprises alternate relationships of exhibition and visitor, and places differing demands on didactics and scenography.

Visual depots

The Porsche Museum in Stuttgart-Zuffenhausen is based on the concept of a "rolling museum": All of the exhibited vehicles are in running condition and thus can be taken to the road anytime. In this sense, the exhibition is always in motion. The museum itself serves as an exclusive depot; its objects sometimes move along the road and are sometimes in a fixed position within the exhibition. As result, the exhibits are still actually vehicles. Each exhibit is presented as a singular object – not as a substitute, but a precious item with very individual aesthetic and narrative characteristics. Similar to the way the building presents itself as a distinctive large-scale sculpture, each exhibit is presented as a sculpture within the interior. Thus, the exhibition design continues the architecture of the building in a congenial way, maintaining an extremely minimal gesture in terms of form, material, and color by emphasizing clear delineation, a limited selection of materials, and mainly the contrast of black and white. It leaves the big show and often colorful appearance to the exhibits. In terms of scenography, the exhibition is divided into three elements, three different stages: a chronologically structured product history, six so-called ideas, and the related thematic arrangements. Simultaneously, these elements comprise topical units with separate subjects, such as "light", "clever, or "intensive". The product history wall, a black gap that runs continuously throughout the entire exhibition space, contains product history and ideas. Its light-absorptive background also serves as an ideal backdrop for the display of exhibits. The six ideas comprise interruptions in the product history chronology. Via table display case, talking image, and research terminal, they illustrate the cardinal virtues and characteristics of corporation and vehicles in a pronounced way. Thematic arrangements and the ideas are joined together in terms of space and content. Examples for this are the protagonists of the 24-hour rallye of Le Mans and the subject "fast", outstanding studies and prototypes and the idea "clever." Generally, the vehicle exhibit remains the focus of all exhibition activity, since all media and textual supplements are designed to be modest and restrained. Only the introductory exhibition unit "Porsche before 1948", the thematic arrangement "Era 917" and the area "How is a Porsche developed" deviate somewhat from this restraint and employ theatrical methods to a stronger degree in order to emphatically illustrate each particular object. Overall however, the scenography of the entire exhibition remains rational. As result, the passion for motor sports, velocity, and attractive delineation of the vehicles becomes the "driving element."

More contemplative, divided into smaller sections, and less loud – which does not mean less passionate – is the character of the Glass Collection of the State Museum of Württemberg in Stuttgart. Here as well, the exhibition design relies on the same principle of reduction and concentration on the exhibit, with necessary modifications. The State Museum of Württemberg purchased the important Glass Collection from Ernesto Wolf in 2003 and thus expanded its own catalog of glass art reaching from the beginnings of classical antiquity into the 19th century. For the presentation of the valuable and fragile exhibits, a cellar with vaulted ceiling below the Dürnitzsaal of the Altes Schloss, the old castle, was made available. Since this space had only served for utilities until now, demolishing and renovation needed to take place in order to create an atmosphere adequate to the collection, in order to have visitors concentrate on the valuable pieces without disturbance. For this purpose, the natural stone walls were patched, the vaulted ceiling stuccoed and glazed, the floors lowered and covered with dark terrazzo and natural stone. The entire space features a low ambient luminosity in order to focus attention on the spotlit exhibits. Further scenographic measures were not necessary in these spaces. Showcases placed in rows, in parallel to the walls, house the exhibits. The showcases, despite their formal quality and precision in craftsmanship, appear to withdraw behind the exhibits and thus refrain from being visually domineering. For this reason, we consider the Glass Collection also as a visual depot that abstains from more elaborate dramaturgy and displays its objects in a discreet and unpretentious way.

We view the third example of the type visual depot in an abstract, yet not rational or content-based continuity to the Porsche Museum and the Glass Collection. From 1936 to 1945 the Sachsenhausen concentration camp served for the training of KZ-commanders and SS staff as well as experimentation grounds for the "perfecting of the KZ-system." Located directly before the gates of Berlin, the former camp is an important place for commemoration and admonition. The total concept of the Sachsenhausen Memorial was awarded the first prize in an international competition and has the goal of regaining awareness of the reality of this place. It displays the totalitarian camp geometry while permitting visitors historic distance and individual interpretation. We designed an abstract, corporeal, protective cover floating above the remnants of the former crematory for the "Station Z" – in the jargon on the camp personnel, the Z as last letter of the alphabet also symbolized the prisoners' "final destination." We perceive an emptiness here that we intended to complete artificially, creating a focus on the interior and thus symbolizing the hopelessness of the prisoners. We feature "Station Z" here, yet we must insist that it comprises a very special case within our work. The goal is not the presentation of an object or an ensemble of objects, even though the crematory also happens to be an object. Rather, but not exclusively, our focus of attention is the

1   Glass collection, State Museum of Württemberg, Stuttgart, 2005
2   Egyptian Courtyard, Neues Museum Berlin, Friedrich August Stüler,
     lithograph based on a watercolor painting by Eduard Gaertner
3–5 Porsche Museum, Stuttgart, 2009; Delugan Meissl Architects,
     exhibition design by hg merz architekten museumsgestalter
6   Glass collection, State Museum of Württemberg, Stuttgart, 2005

6

7

8

particular place, as it is of major significance for crimes committed and remembrance, as well as the immeasurable and unimaginable suffering that prisoners have been subject to in this building complex, in this place. We cannot fathom this suffering in the way we can do so with other, comparatively trivial or profane content in a museum context. It can be experienced, is physically palpable, yet it evades our intellectual grasp despite the available image- and text-based information. The nature of this place resists understanding and comprehension. And this is something we had to acknowledge in our design. Thus, the material remnants receive a protective cover, a translucent PTFE-membrane, affixed to a steel lattice clad in metal grating. It is not a sealed frame; it delimits the space without closing it off hermetically. By doing so it also symbolizes the incomprehensible character of the crimes that have taken place here. The architecture oscillates between openness and closure, proximity and distance, transparency and opacity. We understand it as a device that communicates the impression generated by the interaction of protective cover for defining space, authentic remnants, and the visitor.

Modern chamber of wonders
The modern chamber of wonders constitutes a different kind of museum presentation. We call it modern, as it is scientific, public, and conservationist to a higher, more modern degree than the chambers of wonders of the Renaissance and Baroque. Chambers of wonders used to provide an assembly of objects of all kinds and provenience; rare, exotic, and obscure. Souvenirs from the expeditions of the 15th and 16th century enhanced their wondrous character. Three aspects are characteristic: Firstly, the museum-like collections were created based on a completely heterogeneous enthusiasm for collecting, often beyond systems rooted in science or art history; secondly, these collections were not publicly accessible, but reserved for a privileged audience. Thirdly and finally: These collections were not housed in buildings solely designed as museum buildings, but in private residences, estates of the nobility, or monasteries.

We are the designers for the central exhibition space of the new museum at Bergisel in Innsbruck, and our intention is to turn it into a modern chamber of wonders. By displaying approximately 40 exhibits and/or exhibit ensembles, the 15 m wide and 45 m deep subterranean space provides an unusual and focused insight into the myths and lore of Tyrol. From the beginning, our desire was to enable visitors to experience the size and depth of the space. Thus, we avoided any obstructive interior elements. The order of placement of the exhibits utilizes the entire floor space and is divided into four subject fields, which contain approximately ten exhibit groups each. Decisive for this arrangement is that these groups are not placed in a linear or systematic pattern, but as a dense swarm in which the visitor moves about as a discoverer. The aesthetically appealing objects are thus not ordered according to groups or types, but form diverse ensembles, fragments, archeological excavations of Tyrolean natural, political, and religious history, without wanting to be comprehensive: Natural objects are placed beside cultural records, craftsmanship next to artwork, written documents next to animals and plants. Each visitor has the opportunity to lay out a personal path through the space and discover a personal narrative according to individual interests.

The so-called 6-meter-level in the future Ruhr Museum in Essen follows a similar approach. This level in the former coal washing plant of the Zeche Zollverein displays the history of the Ruhr region following industrialization and the massive transformation from an agrarian region to an extensive industrial landscape, complementing the exhibition units "myth", "phenomena", "structures", "times", and "memory", located on the upper levels within the building. Here as well, exhibit groups of great heterogeneity and density illustrate the introductory talking images and represent a respective era in the form of symbolic and theatrical agglomerations. We consider these also as representatives of the modern chamber of wonders. As in Innsbruck, objects of various origins and types find themselves grouped in a way that expresses the diversity in possible interpretations and the manifold character of industrialization.

Epic museum

We would like to quickly introduce the epic museum as final independent type. Perhaps the title is slightly overpaced, yet the intention should be clear: a museum is epic if it assembles its wealth of objects and narratives within the context of a principle, and by doing so creates a more or less hermetic cosmos, denotes a great narrative.

The Mercedes-Benz Museum in Stuttgart, with its event- and cultural history-oriented exhibition, offers far more than simply lining up historic and recent products next to each other. Instead, it shows which social and cultural significance and dynamics distinguish a brand – a brand that is not only the manufacturer of consumer products but, as a continuously developing institution, constitutes and changes the identity of locations and regions on the one hand and generations of workers, employees, and consumers on the other. Thus, the corporation plays an important role beyond purely economic activity, for instance in culture, sports, or politics. Its inventions and achievements significantly influence the manner in which we are productive, communicative, and mobile within today's global automotive society. The epic and comprehensive character of a museum is articulated by the intention of representing this objective cultural significance in an appropriate way.

For the Mercedes-Benz Museum, we developed the idea of two separate, yet intertwined exhibition vectors in order to do justice to the abundance of exhibits. By taking the unique and extremely extensive collection of vehicles into consideration, the museum features two different modes of presentation: the "Scenes" of the Mercedes Myth and additional visual exhibitions. While the "Myth Spaces" present singular, outstanding vehicles from the product history, the "Collections" serve as visual depots offering room for a variety of diverse utility vehicles and automobiles. On this occasion, however, we would like to focus on the Myth

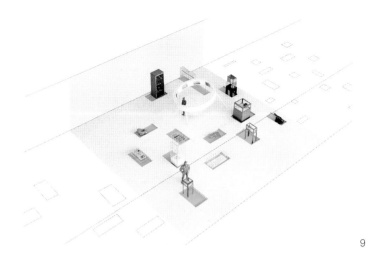

9

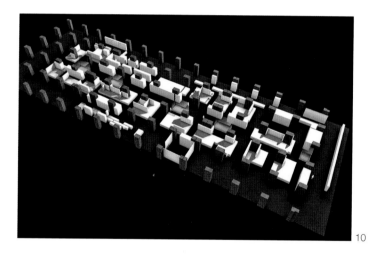

10

11

7–8   "Station Z" Memorial, Sachsenhausen, 2005
9   Bergisel Museum, Innsbruck, 2008
10–11 Ruhr Museum, Essen, 2008

8   Myth 1: 1886–1900
Pioneers: The Invention
of the Automobile

7   Myth 2: 1900–1914
Mercedes: Birth of Brand

6   Myth 3: 1914–1945
Times of Change:
Diesel and Supercharger

5   Myth 4: 1945–1960
Post-War Miracle:
Form and Diversity

4   Myth 5: 1960–1982
Visionaries: Safety and
the Environment

3   Myth 6: since 1982
Moving the World:
Global and Individual

2   Myth 7: Silver Arrows:
Races and Records

1   Foyer: Preshow

0

Collection 1:
Gallery of Voyagers

Collection 2:
Gallery of Carriers

Collection 3:
Gallery of Helpers

Collection 4:
Gallery of Celebrities

Collection 5:
Gallery of Heroes

Fascination of
Technology

12

13

14

Spaces, as these are characterized by the highest degree of complexity in regard to scenography and dramaturgy (ill. 13).

Each Myth Space consists of four repetitive formal elements: Core Wall, Illustrated Timeline, Scene, and Workbench. Room title and text along the Core Wall provide information on the theme and the vehicles. Additionally, large numbers displaying historic dates delimit the particular era of a Myth Space. The Illustrated Timeline is located along the exterior wall of the ramp. It follows a simple principle – to make use of known images of contemporary history. This way, it provides a context for events of corporate history that the general public may not be aware of (ill. 14). The materials used for the Illustrated Timeline are oriented on the historic era of each particular myth. In the Myth Space of the first Mercedes, brass represents the mechanical era. In Myth Space 5, dealing with the subjects of security and ecology, a fabric covering made of airbag material was selected. A "Scene" is installed in the center of each Myth Space and features a particular exhibit, a vehicle with iconic character, such as the first Mercedes from 1901, the famous compressor vehicles from the 1920s and 1930s, or the famous gullwing door cars. By use of combinations of materials and forms, the exhibition dramaturgy lets a particular era resonate within the visitor without evoking that era in an illusionary form. The lesser the historic difference is eroded, the lesser the difference between exhibit and dramaturgy is obscured.

A Workbench is allocated to each Scene, providing in-depth information on technological interrelations (ill. 15). The workbench concentrates on the exceptional technical and design-oriented innovations of the brand such as the compressor and diesel technology, the invention of gullwing doors, or the development of ABS and airbag. These topics are represented in detail via exhibits, text, graphics, and video. Also, a micro-cinema is integrated into Workbenches that summarizes the most important events of the corporate, product, and technology history in a ten-minute film and places these within a greater historic context. The three above-mentioned elements interact and thus perform a play with automotive history as its subject. Only this interaction gives an era a new life that can be experienced in the myth rooms.

What it's really about: spaces of the present
We have seen that exhibition design can lead to completely different modes of presentation and scenography, depending on the subject and configuration of exhibits. It may succeed, but it may also fail – or something in between. However, it should be acknowledged that designers are working on something that, despite being immoveable, is in a transitional phase. As result, the process of designing, similar to e.g. historiography, may change with the methods, possibilities, and tendencies of its time. Which formal dictum and principles it may depend on, if we consider it appropriate or unsatisfactory, at its core the subject is always the same: the creation of contemporaneous spaces.

12–15 Mercedes Benz Museum, Stuttgart, 2006; UNStudio, exhibition
design by hg merz architekten museumsgestalter

Thus, we return to the initial thesis that museums and exhibitions, based on authentic experiencing of objects, create a bridge between present and past, our own or alien cultures and societies. Whether we understand history as progress or decline, we find ourselves – whether we like it or not – within a history of effects that influences us even in our most subtle wishes, expectancies, and actions. We indeed have the liberty whether we deal with this history, retrace the finely woven strands, and let this gained knowledge become part of us. As we all know, this can very well occur without us being aware of it. However, in cases in which we desire to experience and permeate our collective history in a lucid manner, the museum offers us an opportunity to connect with our history, with its focus on the authentic exhibit, i.e. the material remnants of times past. By doing so, the experience within the museum offers a counterpoint to the shrinking of the present within accelerated everyday life and spans open a contemporaneous space of the present in which the past also finds its place. Exhibition design is in the service of this broadening of the present and permits objects to show where they come from and what they are – and thus, also: who we are.

1   Schuster, Peter-Klaus: Das Museum als ästhetische Kirche der Nation. In: Bernhard Maaz (Ed.): Im Tempel der Kunst. Die Künstlermythen der Deutschen. Munich 2008
2   Groys, Boris: Archiv der Zukunft. Das Museum nach seinem Tod. In: Ulrich Borsdorf (Ed.): Die Aneignung der Vergangenheit. Musealisierung und Geschichte. Bielefeld 2004
3   Blom, Philipp: Schafft die Museen ab! In: Die Zeit 02, 2008
4   Figal, Günter: Der Sinn des Verstehens. Beiträge zur hermeneutischen Philosophie. Stuttgart 1996
5   Osten, Manfred: »Alles veloziferisch« oder Goethes Entdeckung der Langsamkeit. Zur Modernität eines Klassikers im 21. Jahrhundert. Frankfurt am Main 2003
6   John, Hartmut: Spielen wir noch in der Champions-League? oder: Plädoyer für professionelle Ausstellungsplanung im Museum. In: Ulrich Schwarz, Philipp Teufel: Museografie und Ausstellungsgestaltung. Ludwigsburg 2001

15

"The Rommel Myth" exhibition in Stuttgart

Architects: Hans Dieter Schaal, Attenweiler

Large photographs on inclined panels, together with other exhibits in angular showcases, shed light on the legend of the German military officer.

53 larger-than-life photographs portraying the Field Marshal and "Desert Fox" Erwin Rommel comprise the core of the temporary exhibition in the Haus der Geschichte of the German state of Baden-Württemberg in Stuttgart.
The exhibition presents items that define the "Rommel myth", each with their individual origin, and embeds them within the respective historic context. Their political, ideological, and cultural functionalization and instrumentalization before and after 1945 thus becomes clear.
On a 500 m² area divided into nine different topical zones, approximately 200 objects documenting the military officer's life and actions are on display. The range of exhibits includes items such as Rommel's field marshal's baton, photo camera, uniforms and medals via family photographs, awards, and newspaper reports to audio documents. The exhibition is however not intended as a place of hero worship, but critically reflects on the legend.

Angled abundance of images
The selected images displayed on the inclined surfaces of the panels seem detached from a greater context.

The panels do not face each other and partially cover each other.
The superimposition of abundant partial images creates, at first glance, a fragmentary overall impression. At closer look however, the large diversity of connections becomes apparent, as well as the continuous repetition of a selected number of core motifs. The exhibition utilizes this abundance of images also to indicate how photos were abused for propaganda purposes. For the exhibition, photos were directly printed onto the surface of MDF panels and fixed in place with bolted connections to their respective positions.
In front of the photos, showcases painted in black and illuminated from within display letters, documents, and battle plans by Rommel.

Projections
The fact that modern media played an important role in the creation of the "Rommel myth" is reflected in the exhibition by use of numerous photos and film sequences. For instance, at the very beginning of the exhibition, visitors are confronted with film projections from the historic "Wochenschau" featuring Rommel's funeral ceremony in the city hall of Ulm. In selected places, text is projected onto photos, indicating what happened in other places while Rommel posed for the photographer.

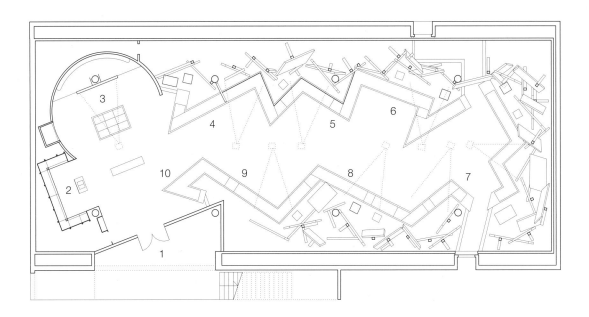

Floor plan
scale 1:250

1 Entrance
2 Biography
3 "State funeral"
4 "Pour le mérite"
5 "Infantry Attacks"
6 "Africa"
7 "Atlantic Wall and resistance"
8 "Forced suicide"
9 "Desert Fox"
10 "Controversial remembrance"

Project Data

Use:	culture/education
Exhibition type:	temporary historic exhibition
Construction:	wood
Clear room height:	4.95 m
Gross volume:	2,376 m³
Exhibition area:	480 m²
Total cost:	€ 230,000 (gross)
Completion:	2008
Construction time:	8 weeks

"That's Opera" traveling exhibition

Architects: ATELIER BRÜCKNER, Stuttgart

The traveling exhibition of the Italian music publisher Ricordi offers visitors a glimpse behind the scenes.

First station of the traveling exhibition, opened in November 2008, was the cultural center "Tour & Taxis" in Brussels. 200 exhibits from the Archivio Ricordi were presented as large-format projections or installations, including hand written scores, letters, as well as stage and costume designs. The exhibition is divided into two topical areas. For one, visitors embark on a round trip through five cube-like spaces, in which the evolution of an opera from libretto to performance is on display. At the same time, between the cubes, the history of the globally renowned music publisher Ricordi is told. A red carpet serves as prologue and leads visitors into the opera's backstage area. The exhibition architecture is oriented on the aesthetics of set design as well as the material selections and level of detail of stage backdrops. Visitors are indeed "backstage", within spaces that are usually not open to them. Columns, scaffolding, cables, and lighting are exposed and increase curiosity for what is inside of the exhibition cubes.

The inspiration for the design of the first exhibition cube "Libretto" is the stage design for the first act of Giacomo Puccini's opera "La Bohème". The artist's attic studio becomes the scriptorium of the librettist. In the second cube "Partitura",

visitors can enter an orchestra pit and listen to the individual choir members, distributed across 42 directional loudspeakers. The handwritten scores are exhibited within showcases in the neighboring soundproof "treasure chamber". The set design studio in the "Scenografia" cube displays model showcases with set designs of renowned operas by Verdi and Puccini. Visitors can individually change the acts with pulleys. The stage set for "Madame Butterfly" is the inspiration for the "Voci e Costumi" cube, featuring Japanese architectural influences in the shape of backlit Shoji-partition elements. The cube houses a second area, the Wardrobe of the Divas. An interactive vanity offers information at the tip of a finger, such as black-white photographs of famous Divas as well as music critics' comments on legendary debut performances. In the last exhibition cube, visitors find themselves in the auditorium of the Scala in Milan. The loggias comprise the background for a spatial installation featuring a 270° video projection, compiling a three-hour performance of Aida into eight minutes. Here, visitors can experience a recent opera dramatization from various perspectives.

A particular challenge for the exhibition designers consisted in modular construction of the exhibition, necessary for being able to travel. The exhibition cubes are comprised of 1 m wide and 3 m tall modules that are clad in different materials. Thus, they can relatively simply be adapted to any exhibition location.

Floor plan
scale 1:500

1 Entrance
2 Prologue
3 Giovanni Ricordi – origins
4 "Libretto"
5 The Ricordi family
6 "Treasure chest"
7 "Partitura"
8 "Scenografia"
9 Ricordi Publishing –
   a modern enterprise
10 "Voci e Costumi"
11 "Rappresentazione"

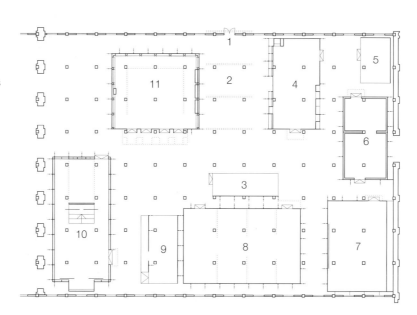

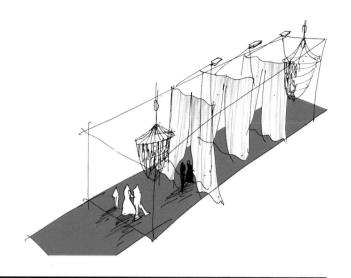

Project data:

Use:	cultural/education
Museum/exhibition type:	works and archive of the Italian music publisher Ricordi
Construction:	wood
Clear room height:	3.5 m
Exhibition area:	1,600 m²
Completion:	2008
Construction time:	3 months

Floor plans • sections
scale 1:200

1 "Libretto"
2 "Treasure chest"
3 "Partitura"
4 "Scenografia"
5 "Voci e Costumi"
6 "Rappresentazione"

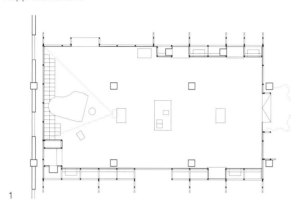

1

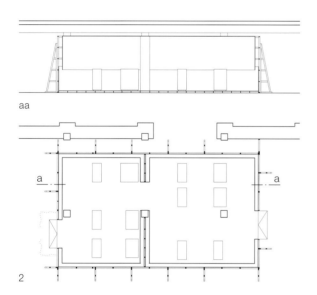

aa

2

bb

3

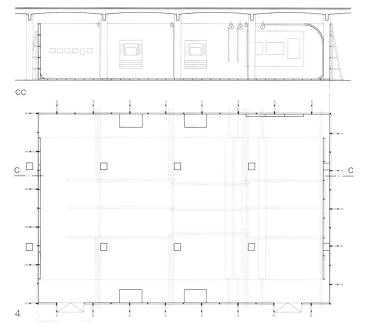

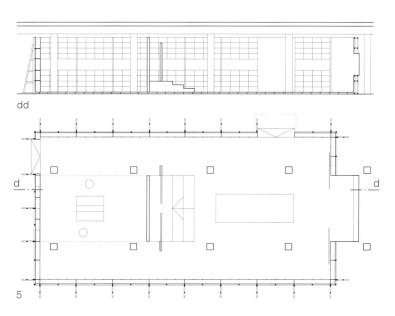

cc

4

dd

5

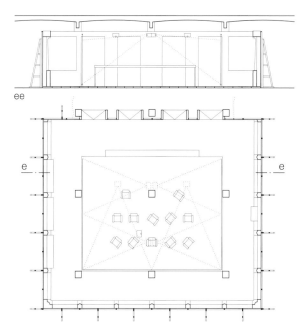

ee

6

Horizontal section • vertical section
seating alcove "Libretto"
scale 1:20

1 spruce cladding, planed, white paint finish 20 mm
2 framing: wood studs (treated for re-use),
   spruce 30/65 mm
3 bookshelf MDF white paint finish 19 mm
4 ornamental door leaf, wood studs (treated for
   re-use), spruce 30/75 mm, Okoumé cladding
   white paint finish 8 mm
5 basic module, wood stud (treated for re-use)
   30/65 mm, mortise/tenon connection
   Okoumé cladding 8 mm
6 framing, seating pedestal: wood studs 50/50 mm,
   spruce cladding white paint finish 15 mm
7 floor construction: floor boards, spruce white
   paint finish 20 mm, particle board 22 mm,
   battens 24/48 mm

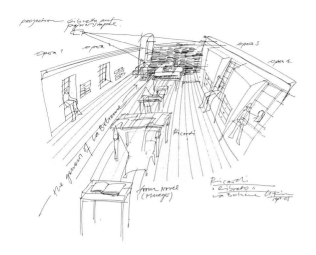

"Inventioneering Architecture" traveling exhibition

Architects: Instant Architecture, Zurich

Project data

Use:	cultural/education
Museum/exhibition type:	architectural traveling exhibition
Construction:	wood
Dimensions:	40/3.5/0.1–1.5 m (l/w/h)
Footprint:	140 m²
Exhibition area:	120 m²
Total cost:	CHF 180,000 (gross)
Completion:	2005
Construction time:	3 months

For two years, this exhibition platform traveled across the world and presented works of four architecture faculties from Switzerland within a spatial sculpture.

When thinking about Switzerland, sensations such as impressive mountain landscapes, deeply blue lakes, exquisite chocolate, and last but not least, spectacular architecture come to mind. This exterior perception provides a topical basis for the joint international traveling exhibition of the architecture faculties of the ETH Zurich, the USI Mendrisio, the EPF Lausanne, and the UNIGE Geneva. By use of urban design models, architectural models, as well as explanatory text, the four universities introduce themselves and illustrate the academic structure of architectural education in Switzerland.

Swiss topography as topic
The basic idea of the exhibition is a cross section through Swiss topography from Zurich via Mendrisio and Lausanne to Geneva. Guided by this concept, Instant Architekten, responsible for the exhibition architecture, developed a 40 m long and 3.5 m wide topographical platform. On one side, the plateau features a mountain ridge – the landscape section, declining to zero across the width of the platform. Visitors can walk upon an exhibition landscape that offers the opportunity for presenting select models, images, and explanatory text,

while simultaneously displaying the origin of the exhibits within the topography. Additionally, each landscape area is labeled with 1 of 4 different colors ranging from light to dark green. The platform not only features exhibits, but in itself becomes a sculpture that defines space. As a whole, the platform comprises a topographical map section in 1:25,000 scale. In relation to an exhibited model in 1:50 scale, it assumes the character of a landscape. For visitors walking on top of it, it is a spatial installation at 1:1 scale.

Construction
A particular challenge consisted in building the platform as cost-efficiently, as light, and as stable as possible to provide for easy assembly and disassembly as well as transport. The complex curved surface consists of individually shaped MDF beams manufactured with a 5-axis milling machine. The entire complex curved surface is made of 1,054 beam elements, each 4 cm wide. In order to define the geometry of the individual surfaces, the manufacturer, "design-to-production", developed a software tool to create polylines based on the curve geometry for the definition of the individual beams. With this data set as basis, all components were manufactured and assembled within a few days.
By use of efficient implementation of this technology, the production cost remained considerably below the initial budget estimate.

Floor plan · section
scale 1:100

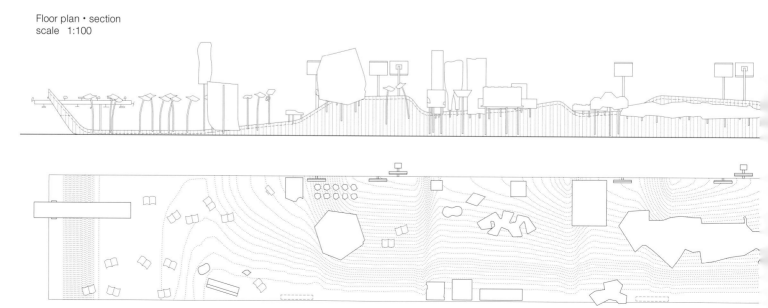

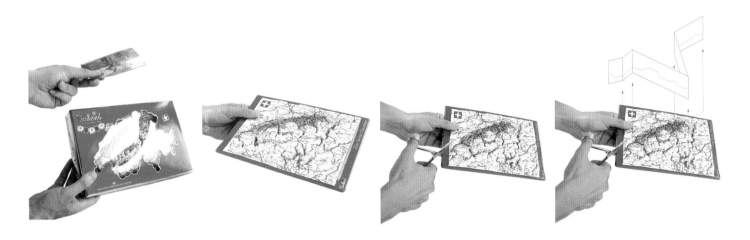

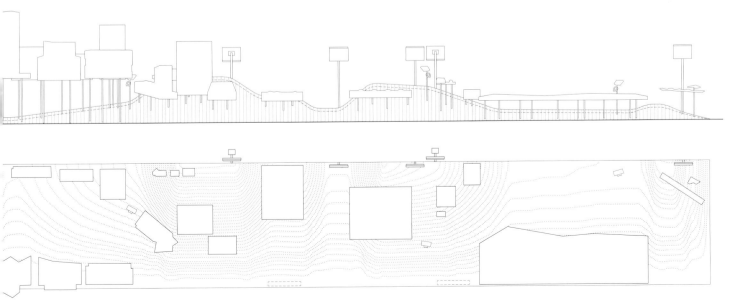

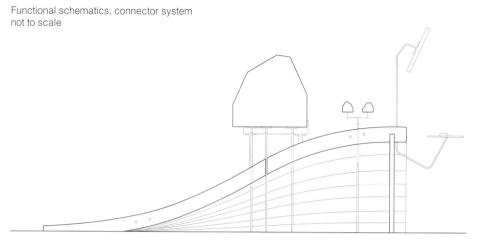

Functional schematics, connector system
not to scale

Museum pavilion in Pouilly-en-Auxois

Architects: Shigeru Ban Architects, Tokyo/Paris;
Jean de Gastines, Paris

The unusual construction of this glazed pavilion along the Canal de Bourgogne offers flexible presentation opportunities.

The Centre d'Interprétation du Canal de Bourgogne is an extensive cultural and art project on the history of this water way located in central France. Along the channel, there are different locations that display different projects. Architects and artists received the call to respond to each particular urban design or landscape context. In Pouilly-en-Auxois, Shigeru Ban created two buildings – a cube-shaped museum pavilion and a vaulted protective roof for a historic canal boat.

Special exhibition spaces
Both buildings are characterized by unconventional construction. The vaulted ceiling of the Hall du Toueur is comprised of cardboard pipes that are connected with aluminum joints and serves as weather protection for the traditional canal boat. The second building, a museum pavilion used for exhibitions and events, resembles a glass cube and is placed directly next to the waterfront promenade where the channel widens into a basin.

Generousness through construction systems
The pavilion includes offices and a space for exhibitions, located in the southern part of the building and comprising approximately two thirds of the available area. The interior features a clear height of 2.90 m and continues visually across the polished screed flooring and the glass facade into the

exterior and up to the bordering water surface. This impression of generousness is made possible by a simple construction system: columns with slender proportions serve for installation of scenography and at the same time are load-bearing elements for the entire ceiling construction. They consist of four perforated and galvanized corner profiles each – standard items as used for industrial storage – which tie into the steel lattice construction of the roof and the floor plate via bolted connections. The compact core featuring restrooms provides structural stiffening of the pavilion.

High flexibility
As the building structure also serves to mount presentation surfaces and spatial partition elements, it withdraws visually and thus leaves the center stage to the exhibition elements. Within the column grid, numerous and flexible opportunities for dividing the space and presenting exhibitions are possible.

Project data:

Use:	cultural/education
Construction:	steel
Clear room height:	2.90 m
Gross volume:	5,015 m³
Gross footprint:	280 m²
Completion:	2004
Construction time:	32 months

Sections · floor plan   scale 1:500
Isometric drawing, construction system

1 Porch/entrance
2 Exhibition
3 Events
4 Restroom core
5 Office

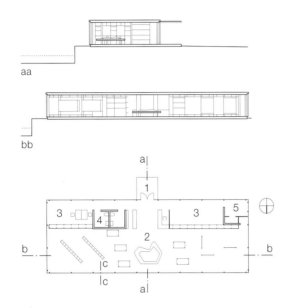

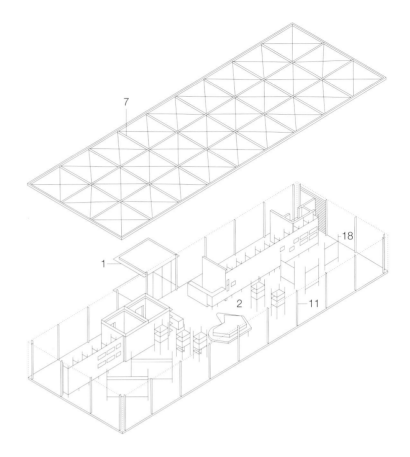

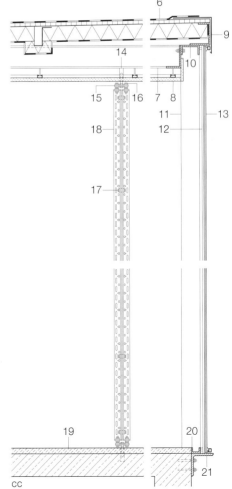

Vertical section   scale 1:20
Blow-up diagram of column   scale 1:10

6 roofing membrane 3 mm
   plywood panels 20 mm
   insulation, mineral wool 80 mm
   vapor barrier 2 mm
   wood blocking, tapered 10–40 mm
7 steel lattice roof structure HEB 120
   steel edge profile ∟120/80/8 mm
8 suspended ceiling, gypsum board 20 mm,
   white finish
9 flashing, canted steel sheet metal
   220/180/2 mm
   steel edge profile ⌐ 70/140/120/8 mm

10 steel channel ⌐ 50/100/8 mm
11 steel facade post ⬭ 100/60/3 mm
12 glass fixture, flat steel ⬭ 10 mm
13 laminated glass 12.8 mm
14 threaded steel pipe Ø 18/50/4 mm
15 flat steel cover 14 mm, threaded rod
16 bolt connection M10
17 bolt connection M8
18 pinned column, 4× steel profile ∟
    40/40/2 mm
19 screed 30 mm
    reinforced concrete slab 120 mm
20 spacer, steel profile ⌐ 30/50/8 mm
21 facade support, continuous steel profile
    ∟120/120/10 mm

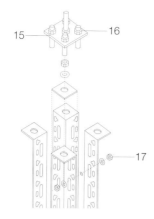

Exhibition pavilion for Artek in Milan

Architects: Shigeru Ban Architects, Tokyo/Paris

aa

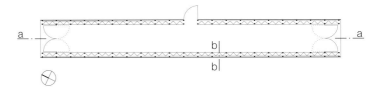

The exhibition pavilion, made of an innovative wood-plastic composite material contributing to resource conservation, can be rebuilt at various locations.

The exhibition pavilion designed by Shigeru Ban for the Finnish design product manufacturer had its debut appearance at the International Furniture Exhibition 2007 in Milan, was later reassembled in Helsinki, and after that presented at Design Miami 2008 in Florida.
The exhibition space, covering nearly 200 m², appears modest yet simultaneously elegant, due to the lightness of the construction and the restrained color selection of the all-white pavilion. Light penetrates the interior through a central transparent roof section.

Material recycling
An innovative wood-plastic composite material is used for construction. The most important basic components of this product are paper and plastic from self-adhesive label production overruns. The composite material is very durable and moisture proof and is appropriate for exterior use without special surface treatment.

The load bearing elements as well as the facades of the pavilion consist of wood-plastic composite L-profiles usually used as corner guards. In order to achieve a stiff load bearing structure, profiles are assembled into truss girders.

Exhibition
At the Milan trade show, the pavilion served as meeting point as well as exhibition pavilion for the company's furniture lines. Shelving for presentation of exhibits was integrated into the pavilion structure. The restrained design enables emphasizing the presentation of exhibited objects that can thus impressively display their colors and shapes before the white background of the pavilion.

Project data:

Use:	cultural/education
Construction:	wood-plastic composite material
Clear room height:	5.88 m
Gross volume:	830 m³
Gross footprint:	185 m²
Total cost:	€ 250,000 (gross)
Completion:	2007
Construction time:	2 weeks

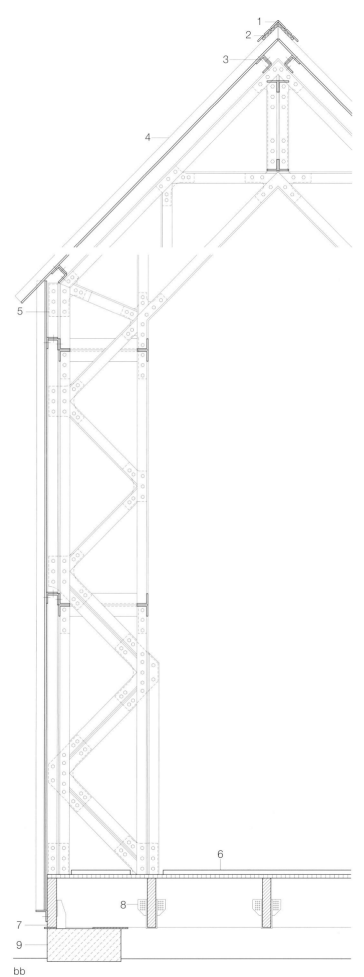

Section · floor plan   scale 1:500
Vertical section   scale 1:20

1 L-profile, wood-plastic composite 60/60/8 mm
   + 2× wood-plastic composite strips 60/8 mm on
   both sides
2 rubber liner
3 2× L-profile, wood-plastic composite
   60/60/8 mm, ⊔-configuration (bolted)
4 standard L-profile, wood-plastic composite
   60/60/8 mm
5 all connections: flat steel 2 mm
6 floor board, wood-plastic composite 25 mm
   plywood panels 18 mm
7 wood beam 45/260 mm
8 joist hanger
9 concrete masonry units

LIGHT
DOES
NOT
ILLUMINATE,
IT
TELLS
A
STORY.
LIGHT
GIVES
MEANINGS,
DRAWS
METAPHORS
AND
SETS
THE
STAGE
FOR
THE
COMEDY
OF
LIFE.
ETTORE SOTTSASS

Built Identity
Architecture – Design – Communication

Jons Messedat

Built identity equals responsibility

Corporate architecture is built identity – for the analogous encounter of corporations, people, and brands. Its challenge consists in communicating a corporate message and values in a way that all senses of perception are addressed, thus enabling people to see, feel, and perhaps even listen to architecture. This particular spatial quality of experience can never be replaced by the virtual spaces and artificial worlds of the Internet. They can, at best, supplement them.

High quality architecture generally is the result of a collaborative partnership between architects and enthusiastic companies as clients. Names such as Walther Rathenau, Adriano Olivetti, Philip Rosenthal or Rolf Fehlbaum and Berthold Leibinger, to name a few, represent a way of building that embodies built identity in a sustainable way. Being generally open-minded towards independent and sometimes visionary architecture has always paid off for corporations, despite pragmatic arguments for cost effectiveness. A credible spatial identity however not only has the potential to contribute to commercial success, but also reflect the responsibility of clients within corporate citizenship. Against the background of uncertainty and loss of trust in some lines of business, it has become a special challenge for corporations today to use temporary and permanent construction projects to display credibility. Within this context, aspects such as authenticity and sustainability are no short-lived slogans, but comprise a new challenge in translating content and values into spatial identity.

Built corporate identity – milestones

The objective of corporations to adequately present themselves through temporary buildings at trade shows or their office headquarters is not without precedent. In the transition from unique handicraft to reproducible mass item, not only products themselves, but also modes of presentation, as well as the architecture of production facilities have changed. At first, the founding fathers of the industrial dynasties superimposed historicist shells onto their highly modern production facilities. The new possibilities of industrial design became architecturally apparent only much later. A much-cited contribution to this development was the strategic alliance between AEG, under the leadership of Walther Rathenau, and the self-taught designer Peter Behrens. After his appointment as art counselor, Behrens developed a comprehensive design concept for the company, encompassing graphics, products, and architecture, thus setting a long-lasting standard. In today's words, he would have been the first brand manager, whose work carries traits of what would be called corporate design only much later.

The influence of early Modernist architecture on corporations became specifically apparent in the collaboration between Walter Gropius and Carl Benscheidt, the owner of shoe last producer Fagus, located in Alfeld on the Leine. The manufacturer was open for the architect's innovative suggestions and in 1911 contracted Gropius to contribute as architectural designer to the production building already under construction at that time. The steel and glass facades of the Fagus Works were used for the company's entire communication campaign, e. g. catalogs and advertisement, and generated an enormous degree of recognition for both the building as

2

3

well as its owner. A very successful and, even today, effective "branding", to use a term of contemporary marketing.

In a number of successful cases, the sum of corporate and design visions led to a networking of cultural activity, groundbreaking presentation concepts, and seminal architecture. In Italy for instance, the typewriter manufacturer Olivetti took over the role of cultural spearhead by employing avantgarde designers, architects, and artists. The epochal design of products, but also of showrooms and corporate buildings, turned the company into a cultural magnet of its time. Adriano Olivetti created a network of cultural institutions, founded the INU (Instituto Nazionale di Urbanistica), and supported publications and exhibitions. Later, under the supervision of the Austrian designer Hans von Klier, a unified corporate identity design was created for Olivetti. Within the so-called red books, a mandatory design for all communication tasks was determined – an early example of a comprehensive corporate design manual.

Corporate design – unity and diversity

At the Hochschule für Gestaltung in Ulm (HfG) in Germany, the fields of graphic design, photography, typography, and exhibition design were combined for the first time into a combine study course called "visual communication". For Otl Aicher, the goal in collaborating with corporations consisted in comprehensively designing, if possible, all forms of communication, from the letterhead to the exhibition stand.

Since then, corporate design manuals have been used most of all by the so-called global players in order to produce a globally valid brand appearance. Here, unified design characteristics are determined for all visual components of corporate presence, to achieve a ubiquitous recall value of locations. The individual designer and individual design elements vanish into the background. The spatial media of architecture however seems less important within this model of dominating typography and color-coding. On the one hand, strict corporate design guidelines offer the opportunity to guarantee continuity and affiliation by formulating binding design standards. However, the danger exists that no sufficient freedom is left for individual, regionally diverse, and perhaps even surprising presentation concepts. Most of all commercial areas, shopping malls, and shopping centers are, to a large degree, defined by the standard design of global chain store operators and are becoming more and more uniform. In most cases, an effective advertisement sign is sufficient to awaken expectations, met according to precisely defined patterns. Thus, the question arises if corporate design can, in the long term, contribute to a dynamic development of corporations or instead become a handicap for vivid corporate identities.

Corporate architecture as process

Individual places and spaces that respond to both their context and regional challenges comprise an answer to a progressing uniformity of system-oriented visual appearances. Corporate architecture thus becomes an instrument for differentiation in competition and can assume surprising and sometimes even avantgardistic appearances. More and more people have become aware of this in recent years. Also, the scope of tasks covered by both architecture and corporate architecture has, by now, significantly increased. The tasks

4

that architects are confronted with here in the context of a holistic design process have often developed into distinct interdisciplinary fields of expertise. However, this was and is also necessary, due to increasing requirements in construction projects that have become more and more complex. In addition, there are less and less individual industrialists who are also critical clients interested in discussing architecture. Instead, in larger, non-owner operated companies, decisions are filtered through numerous levels of hierarchy.

The most important decisions that contribute to success or failure of projects are made in the very beginning, even before particular planning has actually taken place. This is the time when clients and all planning partners should agree on a basic gesture that comprehensively pervades the entire planning process. The freedom for setting the course for all steps to follow is greatest at the very beginning. At the same time, the follow-up costs for conceptual changes are the lowest. Exactly this is where the concept for a comprehensively planned corporate architecture should set in.

At the beginning of the joint planning process, detailed research and analysis of the current conditions should take place, as well as an analysis of how the corporation perceives itself and is perceived by others. Also, setting up an interdisciplinary design group that supervises the entire process has proven successful in the past. Basic demands such as core values and future positioning need to be detected, determined, and compiled into a guiding principle that is binding for all planning partners and serves as orientation. Key phrases formulate far-sighted, superordinate objectives that simplify the day-to-day communication between clients and employees. First, in order to communicate central ideas and future goals, it is necessary to summarize them briefly. This provides a basis for internal communication, for the construction of prototypes, and the contracting of external planners as well as organizing optional competitions.

In order to guarantee the goal of a comprehensive corporate architecture in a sustainable way, it is necessary to repeatedly review common topics and also reassess them. This does not imply deviating from long-term goals. Instead, it is proof of a dynamic and vivid corporation and brand.

Formats from S to XXL
Brand values continuously increase. Thus, it is no surprise that corporate architecture for industry and trade is gaining importance. More and more corporations recognize the opportunities and markets that can be accessed by use of built identity. The scope of spatial communication tasks reaches from exhibition stands to brand spaces and urban scale master plans. Until now, mostly producers of brand products have invested significantly into their spatial identity. Lately, small and medium size businesses and regional associations as well recognize the added value of an independent and high quality corporate architecture. Most of all clients who are traditionally firmly rooted in their location can contrib-

5

1   Zumtobel Light Forum, Dornbirn, 2005; Herbert Resch, Aysil Sari
2   Fagus Works, Alfeld on the Leine, 1914; Walter Gropius, Adolf Meyer
3   Fagus Works, exhibition on the history of the shoe last manufacturer
4   Olivetti showroom, New York, 1954; BBPR
5–6 Hilti Brand World, Schaan, 2007; Triad Berlin

6

7

ute to the subject of built identity in an excellent way. In this case, the precise analysis of regional conditions, traditions, and product philosophies comprises a solid basis for the definition and implementation of a new architecture, typical for its respective region. For the public, the expansion of communication into the third dimension creates new vantage points for recognizing corporate culture, corporate philosophy, and local ways of life.

Brand exhibitions and competence centers

The sheer amount of information and technical details of products and services of all kinds increases day by day and can now be accessed at any time and from everywhere. By entering only a single search word, the World Wide Web almost immediately offers a global overview of the object of interest. When corporations and their customers meet, an increased amount of up-to-date detail knowledge is available that can be considered common knowledge for product presentations and in consultations. For corporations it therefore becomes more and more important to present their unique selling proposition and performance characteristics in an applied form within brand exhibitions and competence centers. While technical aspects are communicated online in two-dimensional form, corporate architecture can demonstrate these aspects three-dimensionally. For businessmen, invitations to corporate office headquarters are an opportunity to guide visiting customers according to their own concept. Thus, at an in-house event, opposed to public trade shows, the audience can be addressed exclusively and in a targeted way. According to the line of business and related goals, different modes of presentation can be implemented here.

In-house exhibitions are suitable especially for presenting new products or seasonal product lines. Here, deals and consultations with customers and distribution partners can take place, and they can be made familiar with recent innovations and tendencies. In an ideal case, a topical framework complements the program, e.g. with lectures, exhibitions, or panel discussions. Brand exhibitions offer the opportunity to convey more information on the historic background and the core values of a brand. These are closely tied together with the on-site corporate tradition and supplement the production facilities, developed over time, with documentary and museum-oriented functions. The proximity of production and product can lead to intriguing spatial juxtapositions and surprising insights into the host's opus moderandi. For instance, product-related materials and elements typical for the corporation can be integrated into the spatial appearance on site. Competence centers can be used for conferences and are also aimed at corporate employees who have the opportunity to become acquainted with their employer's objectives. Transitions between different presentation and communication techniques can be seamless. What unites them all is the desire to not only characterize a corporation through branding, but also become familiar with it on site. A dedicated architectural context is created that can, in the long run, lead to a reallocation of marketing budgets, from exhibition participation to investments in the corporate headquarters.

Flagship stores and supermarkets

In the past years, an obvious polarization within conceptualizing and designing new consumer environments has become apparent. While premium brands produce spectacular archi-

8

tectural gestures in metropolitan city centers, items such as food and other everyday products are purchased in shopping centers at the urban fringe, at the lowest possible price. We have the hedonistic shopping culture of flagship stores on the one hand, and on the other the pragmatic discount boxes located in the great wide open.

The products of different producers are no longer offered at their point of sale, placed side by side in rows, but each in a separate architectural context. Sellers predominantly in the premium segment tend to take the distribution of their products into their own hands, in order to guarantee quality standards and to protect their brand value from production to purchase. Also, rebates and sales are anathema to producers of brand items. After all, price stability guarantees long term product value retention. The trend towards single brand stores, for instance in the fashion business, has increased significantly, while owner-operated stores that offer various labels are struggling for survival. Flagship stores offer the necessary space for a brand's entire product selection and the envisioned diversification of portfolios through associated product lines. At present, accessories for instance occupy more and more space, and as result, producers of exclusive travel baggage also offer fashion or arts and crafts, and stationery manufacturers also sell watches and jewelry. In European cities, the representations of big brand names are mostly integrated into an historic context that has developed over time. In Tokyo however, premium brands indulge in building spectacular flagship stores that dominate entire streetscapes and urban quarters. Thus, in the past years, the famous Omotesando, located in the exclusive Aoyama-District, has changed into a prestige boulevard for premium brands with spectacular buildings by the international architectural avantgarde. At the same time, the typical design signatures of some architects have become a brand of their own, an effective means of advertisement in this context. Thus it is possible that very similar architectural shapes are used in different parts of the world for very different clients in arts and commerce. The more such an "image provider" however is used, the less effective the desired impression becomes.

Until recently, giant parking lots and an equally extensive range of merchandise were the cutting edge in attracting customers within the competition between supermarkets. There had already been attempts in reinvigorating the visual impression of these "decorated sheds", such as the shopping centers of the American BEST brand, which received aesthetic camouflage via artistic interventions in the 1970s. Until now, supermarket design implied that merchandise could be offered at such inexpensive prices most of all through absence of quality of space.

Lately however individual supermarket chains try to prove the opposite. An equally striking and high quality design can both serve to improve aesthetic and functional aspects as well as increase profit. Once again, good architecture that takes regional requirements, materials, and consumer de-

9

10

7 Kaldewei showroom, Ahlen, 2005; Bolles + Wilson
8 Zumtobel Light Forum, Dornbirn, 2005; Herbert Resch, Aysil Sari
9 Prada Aoyama Epicenter, Tokyo, 2003; Herzog & de Meuron
10 Freitag flagship store, Zurich, 2006; Spillmann Echsle Architekten

mands into account has become an object of interest. Spaces are created for the presentation of items that are, for instance, not hermetically sealed consumer environments, but relate to the exterior by simple means such as introducing daylight and natural ventilation. Most of all in Austria innovative impulses for new supermarkets are on the rise. The Tyrolean regional grocery chain MPreis for instance has championed the notion that a superordinate vision can be achieved economically, also with individual buildings. In the meantime, the necessity for high quality corporate architecture and merchandise presentation has also led to intriguing retail environments worldwide. The concepts are quite distinct and no unified formula for this significant improvement in quality can be identified. Good for the customers, since shopping can be fun again and may once more become a true (spatial) experience, also in supermarkets.

11

Brand environments and factory museums

The most spatially expansive brand statements finally are brand environments that may even become as big as urban design projects. Different functions such as shopping, entertainment, and cultural services are merged into large-scale attractors. These places in the service of brands constitute the spatial context for discovering the corporation and its products. Here, aspects such as tradition, competence, and corporate philosophy are dramatized spatially. Complex compositions of architecture, graphics, media, and exhibits make the invisible background of brands visible in order to build an imaginary environment for the immersion of visitors. Thus, semi-public spaces are created that not only appeal to customers but also provide space for events in an often breathtaking ambiente.

In the past years, most of all the automotive industry has created spectacular brand environments in order to position themselves in the global market place. The goal is to materialize and capture the thrill of speed in the shape of unmistakable buildings. The distinction between their construction and the products on display has nearly vanished. Thanks to state-of-the-art software, architectural shapes can be generated today that embody completely new kinds of "bodywork". Transitions from floor, to wall, to ceiling merge into a continuous flow that lets visitors hover through spaces, augmented by media. Scenographically designed factory museums contribute new approaches to classical, object-oriented presentation concepts in which exhibits are placed on display and documented.

Just as art enthusiasts no longer visit museums in order to see rows and rows of objects, customers today expect more than a simple display of products. Virtual and augmented spaces and installations complement real-time content and enable dynamic forms of presentation. Today, strategic partnerships between protagonists in culture and science dismantle the barriers between museography and brand presentation.

New challenges and perspectives

Identity is a central topic in developing presentations, places, and spaces that are in the service of corporations and brands. Only unique places and spaces that establish identity, create tension, and embody a narrative, have recall value. The French ethnologist and anthropologist Marc Augé combines

12

these aspects critically within his theory of spaces and non-spaces: "Places and spaces are characterized through identity, relation, and history. Equally so, a space without identity and which neither can be described as relational or historic, defines a non-space. Today, more than often non-spaces are created..."[1] But how can a space that doesn't correspond to a particular client become an unmistakable address?

Branding

The future user often isn't even determined yet when construction begins, and elements that establish identity can only be integrated after the fact. In this case, the place itself needs to assume the function of a built brand in order to be perceived in a positive light by both the targeted user group as well as the public. Here, architecture can become the decisive criterion of distinction, providing a clear definition within the market. Thus, most of all when considering the mass of anonymous office and commercial spaces, corporate architecture becomes a new challenge in project development.

The formulation of a concept serves as basis, both relating to the location as well as future changes. The placement of, for instance, an unmistakable name, the development of flexible spatial concepts, as well as a striking spatial materialization comprise elements of this concept. Far-sighted planning that responds to dynamic processes of change influences long-term operational costs in a positive way. Buildings that are exclusively tailored to a single user due to superimposed branding often need to be neutralized with significant expenditure when users change. In the future, project development will also need to offer more than the provision of an ideal technical and economic infrastructure. The goal is to anchor a core within the built reality that conveys sustainability and credibility.

Sustainability

Subjects such as climate and environmental protection and the conservation of natural resources increasingly become central issues in society. The most recent trigger for a process of reassessment was the G8 summit in June 2007 in Heiligendamm with the motto "Growth and Responsibility". For the first time, climate protection, along with new demands regarding energy, water, and resources conservation were on top of the agenda.

These new objectives have also reached the construction industry: at the leading trade show of the real estate industry, the MIPIM in Cannes, a prize is awarded in the category "Green Building". Green building and green design are the new key topics in innovative construction and design concepts intended as contribution to climate protection. The concept of green building determines the resource efficiency of buildings in order to reduce detrimental effects on human health and the natural environment. In the past years, various national and international green building certifications have been established. For instance, the responsible institution in England, the Building Research Establishment, provides the BREEAM certification. In the USA, the LEED (Leadership in

13

11 MPREIS, Wenns, 2001; Rainer Köberl, Astrid Tschapeller
12 Interspar, Rum, 2005; ATP Architekten und Ingenieure
13 Porsche Museum, Stuttgart, 2009; Delugan Meissl Architekten

14

Energy and Environmental Design) label of the U.S. Green Building Council is the prominent equivalent. Beginning 2009 in Germany, the certification "Nachhaltiges Bauen" (sustainable building) of the DGNB (German Association for Sustainable Building) was awarded for the first time. It is regarded a second generation system as it includes all aspects of sustainable building in its evaluation, including ecological and economic factors, as well as sociocultural and functional aspects, process quality, technical quality, and quality of location. All of these systems are oriented towards the objective of establishing a positive trademark for verifiable environmental awareness.

The opportunities for improving resource conservation are significant: After all, buildings of all kinds contribute to about 50 % of primary resource consumption and cause almost 40 % of emissions and 25 % of waste volume. Green building standards are thus more than short-term reactions to climate change and rising energy costs. In order to improve the way we deal with our planet's limited resources, an all-encompassing paradigm change is necessary. "Carry on" is something we can no longer afford, neither in ecological nor economic terms. The global shortage and rise in cost of resources will, in the long run, determine the economic success of corporations. Intelligent concepts for natural resource conservation guarantee a significant competitive advantage. This regards temporary buildings at trade shows and exhibitions as well as buildings for long-term use. In the future, corporations, investors, and designers whose corporate architecture is not oriented towards aspects of sustainability will have a hard time convincing both the public and their customers of their credibility.

Authenticity

Credibility, dependability, and realness are possible translations of the classical Greek term authentikos. A person described as authentic seems particularly real, i.e. the person conveys a self-image that is perceived as real and not artificial. The person's entire appearance seems authentic when rational and emotional, verbal and non-verbal, visible and invisible signals and information match. The label "authentic" fits products, brands, and spaces that provide us with the impression that they are in fact "themselves" and thus credible, dependable, and real. Abraham Lincoln once said, "Perhaps a man's character was like a tree, and his reputation like its shadow; the shadow is what we think of it, the tree is the real thing."[2]

Corporations invest significantly into their appearance and thus into how they are perceived on a secondary level. However, it is equally important to design the corporate personality itself, i.e. the corporate reality. For corporations, authenticity means that corporate ways of acting are not defined by external influences and manipulations, but reflect their own values and standards. These standards are valid for the actions of the corporation as a whole and for internal and external communication means and content. A particular

15

14 Meilenwerk classic car forum, Düsseldorf, 2006;
   RKW Architektur + Städtebau
15 Meydan shopping center, Istanbul, 2007; Foreign Office Architects
16 Roche Forum conference center, Buonas, 2002;
   Scheitlin-Syfrig + Partner

challenge in spatial communication consists in conveying these central values in an authentic way. This doesn't imply making a corporation simply appear as if it acts in an authentic way. A "dramatized" authenticity quickly loses credibility when the public discovers that a corporation does not act internally as it promises externally concerning sensitive issues. Whoever wants to be credible in the future needs to engage in a true dialog in order to continuously enable customers to trust them and also sustain this trust.

Added value through built identity

High-quality construction projects for corporations are the outcome of numerous singular procedural steps and farsighted decisions, the direction of which is determined by a joint objective. A coherent representation today encompasses much more than the design of visible elements of physical appearance. The goal is to produce a gesture that defines binding standards for an entire corporate appearance. Aspects such as sustainability, authenticity, and acceptance will, in the future, assume a far greater role in spatial communication. The identity of individuals and their living conditions and personal circumstances are continuously influenced by new local and global parameters. Fractures, interferences, blur, and diffusion have become a part of daily life. Perhaps it would be interesting to take these aspects into account more emphatically in the future. The postulate of singularity should however not be perceived as a carte blanche for an arbitrary stance. Basis for a convincing transformation of corporate content into architecture is always sound thematic positioning. This can however not be result of top-down decisions, but can only be established in a procedural, open, and (self-)critical dialog between all participating partners.

We need to remember two things: Corporate architecture is only truly sustainable when the corporation's attitude and its spatial implementation correspond. And in the context of increasing vacancy of anonymous commercial and retail real estate, it certainly isn't a mistake to create a really good and credible address.

1 Augé Marc: Orte und Nicht-Orte. Frankfurt 1994
2 Fehrenbacher, Don and Fehrenbacher, Virginia (eds.): Recollected Words of Abraham Lincoln. Stanford 1996: 43

Further reading:
Brauer, Gernot: Dynaform + Cube – Architecture as Brand Communication. Basle 2002
Birkigt, Klaus et al.: Corporate Identity – Grundlagen, Funktionen, Fallbeispiele. Landsberg am Lech 1995
Jaeggi, Annemarie: Fagus – Industrial Culture from Werkbund to Bauhaus. New York 2000
Kicherer, Sybille: Olivetti – A Study of the Corporate Management of Design. New York 1990
Messedat, Jons: Corporate Architecture – Development, Concepts, Strategies. Basle 2005
Messedat, Jons: Flagship Stores – Shops, Showrooms, Brand Centers. Ludwigsburg 2007
Messedat, Jons: Architekten als Markenbildner – gebaute Unternehmenskultur. In: Der Neue Architekt – Erfolgreich am veränderten Markt. Munich 2008
Messedat, Jons: Schnittstellenkompetenz gefragt – Corporate Architecture schafft »gebaute Markenidentität«. In: Corporate Design 2008. Perspektiven – Auszeichnungen – Profile. Bonn 2008
Riewoldt, Otto: Brandscaping – Worlds of Experience in Retail Design. Basle 2002
Wines, James: SITE. New York 1989

16

Audi Center in Munich

Architects: Allmann Sattler Wappner, Munich

Site plan
scale 1:4,000

Dynamics, asymmetry, and transparency are the major design characteristics of Audi's new Corporate Identity Architecture.

The primary motivation for the further development of Audi's Corporate Architecture is based in increased area requirements for the continuously growing product line as well as a strengthened brand presence in international metropolitan centers.

The architectural concept is intended to meet the spatial and functional demands of automotive dealership as well as requirements of brand communication. An architectural vocabulary with comprehensive typology and striking visual appearance was needed for very heterogeneous locations. In terms of construction and space, concepts had to be organized flexibly, based on a modular system, and easily scalable. Thus, a cube-shaped spatial enclosure was developed, intersected by a banked track on each floor, reflected in the facade design. This way, different functions such as e.g. new and pre-owned car sales can be spatially separated from one another. The facade apertures can vary according to urban context and thus provide for a diverse, yet globally recognizable architectural gesture. Car showrooms are scheduled to open in Las Vegas, Los Angeles, Tokio, and Dubai, among others.

Audi Center Munich as prototype

The Audi Center Munich is the first completed project in Germany based on the Corporate Identity Architecture concept. The building is completely enclosed in a shell made of silver colored, perforated, and canted aluminum sheet metal. The glazed apertures reaching from floor to ceiling seem similar to incisions within the homogeneous overall appearance, permitting gracious views of the building's interior and the exhibited vehicles. The window soffits follow the geometry of the interior banked track.

Dynamic interior architecture

New vehicles are placed along two levels connected by a gracious escalator. The horizontal arrangement of spaces permits presenting numerous vehicles on a comparatively small plot in the urban core.

The interior space is mainly characterized by the two banked tracks that define the exhibition area and spatially separate the auxiliary areas. Presented vehicles are placed freely along the curved surface of the wall. Spotlights integrated into the walls effectively illuminate the exhibits. A freely placed furniture element serves as reception desk and service counter. The customer service zone is located on the lower level behind the curved walls; lounge, café, and shop are situated on the upper level. Views of the exhibition areas provide orientation and create a spatial impression of openness. With their restrained color selection in black, grey, and white, interior surfaces provide the space with a cool atmosphere.

The customer vehicle pick-up is located in the eastern section of the building, contrasting the exhibition spaces in terms of color and material. It features translucent white Plexiglas panels with metal framing and facing comprised of reflective material. Light fixtures placed within the gap between acrylic glass and rear facing illuminate the space with brilliant white light.

Project data:

Use:	showroom for cars/retail
Construction:	steel
Clear room height:	6 m (exhibition areas)
	3 m (auxiliary areas)
Gross volume:	22,300 m³
Gross footprint:	4,100 m²
Exhibition area:	1,200 m²
Total cost:	€ 10 million
Completion:	2008
Construction time:	12 months

A The interplay of the different requirements of functional areas determine the interior organization of the building. The large circles represent new and pre-owned car sales.
B Implementation of multi-story organization of buildings

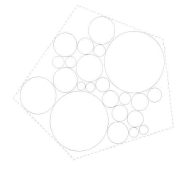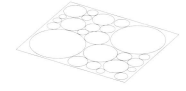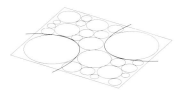

A   exterior and interior influences   footprint   separations

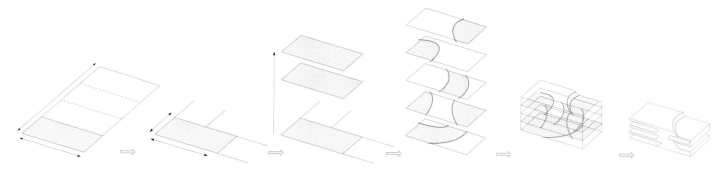

gross usable area, single-story Audi Center	footprint, urban context	multi-story organization	multi-story organiza-tion of sales floors	spatial layering	complete Audi Center

B

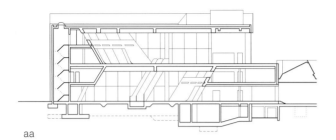

aa

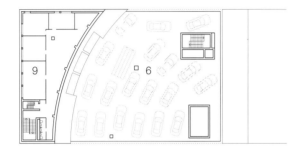

Section · floor plans
scale 1:750

1 Reception
2 Waiting lounge
3 Sales floor
4 Customer service
5 Vehicle pick-up
6 Void
7 Lounge/cafeteria
8 New vehicle sales
9 Office

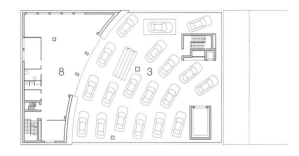

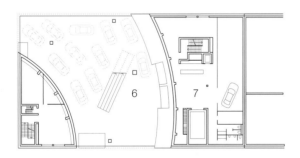

Vertical section
banked track
scale 1:20

10 reinforced concrete 400 mm
11 suspended ceiling, gypsum board 12.5 mm
   acoustic perforation 6/18 R, acoustic fleece
12 aluminum sheet metal facing, canted edge,
   paint finish 25/350/50 mm
13 parapet:
   finish epoxy resin, stucco 15 mm
   reinforced concrete 420 mm
14 recessed floodlight, turn- and tiltable
   casing, steel sheet metal, painted finish
15 floor construction:
   stoneware tile 10 mm
   adhesive layer 7 mm
   cement screed 95 mm
   PE-foil separation layer
   impact sound proofing, wood wool 20 mm
   PE-foil separation layer
   insulation, foam glass panels 100 mm
   sealant, reinforced concrete slab 300 mm

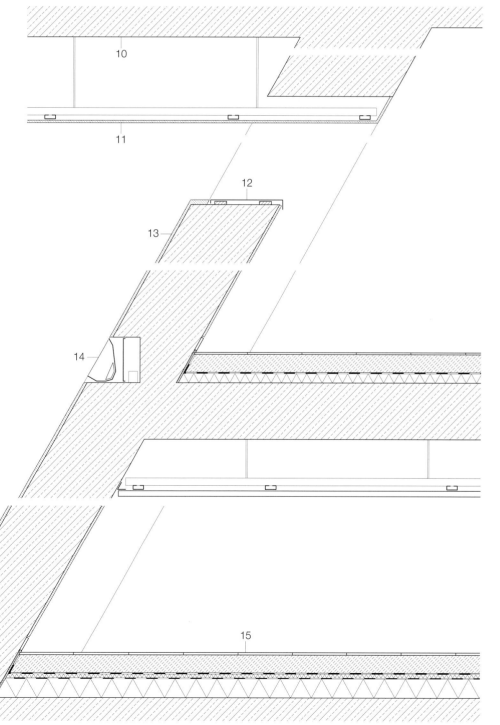

adidas Brand Center in Herzogenaurach

Architects: querkraft Architekten, Vienna

This brand environment, completely dedicated to sports, features large-scale projections and showrooms within a clearly defined building volume.

The shoemaker Adi Dassler's incredible success story began in Herzogenaurach in the 1920s. Today, the now second largest sports equipment manufacturer worldwide dominates the small town in the German region of Franconia: Either in the city center or at its fringes, the brand is omnipresent – as outlet store, administrative building, in sports activities, or within the stores in the small pedestrian area. In 1997 the available spaces in the city center became insufficient, so the company looked for a suitable location for their headquarters, including corporate administration, residential area, public infrastructure, and commercial zones. In 1999 a former air base covering 114 hectares located at the outskirts of the city was selected as new location. The Brand Center was added as central element of the location in 2006.

Timeless exterior, changing times within the interior

The Brand Center comprises a shining black building volume with a footprint of 170 by 70 m. It assumes its position within the surrounding landscape as if it had always been there. This is due to the fact that part of the building is hidden below grade. The glazed reflective facade makes the building vanish into its surrounding, and as result it is difficult to view in its entire length. At night, the effect is reversed and

the shell, visually impenetrable at day, is transformed into a vividly lit storefront. Visitors enter the building at the highest point of the foyer. It is simultaneously point of access and initial presentation space – the "arena". Its generous steps are reminiscent of a stadium and follow the outline of an interior cube-shaped volume with expansive surfaces. 25 beamers continuously project images onto the upper area of its 135 m long concrete wall projection surface, introducing the adidas brand world. Within its interior, the corporation displays retail concepts and product lines in the "working area". The individual areas of exhibited product lines are separable by light sliding walls that can also open up the entire length of the space if required. This flexibility is continued into the conference rooms that can be connected if necessary.

Construction

After completing the floor slab and the perimeter walls below grade, the entire building was assembled from prefabricated components. The secondary roof girders are completely prefabricated. The primary roof girders were delivered in segments and assembled on site. Diagonal columns serve as cross-bracing and provide structural stiffening. In order to keep the sharp-edged, rigid glass shell free of movement created by heat expansion in the roof, facade and roof can be detached by a hydraulic mechanism. At the same time, the delicate shell transmits strong wind loads into the roof structure. The diagonal columns stiffen the entire construction, and as result movements of facade members are reduced.

Project data:

Use:	brand and product presentation
Construction:	steel, exposed concrete
Clear room height:	7.70 m ("arena")
	5.60 m (forum and "working area")
Gross volume:	93,000 m³
Gross footprint:	12,492 m²
Exhibition area:	1,950 m² ("arena")
	300 m² ("walk of fame")
	5,200 m² ("working area")
Completion:	2006
Construction time:	12 months

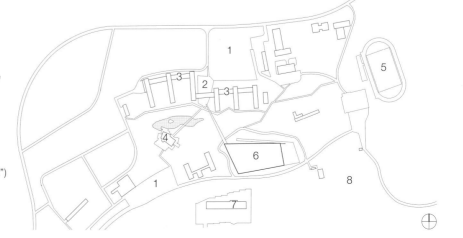

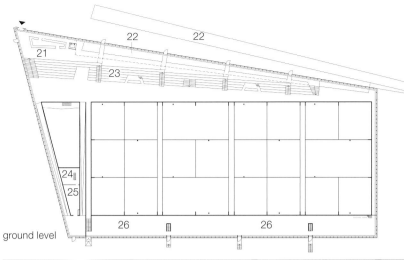

ground level

Site plan
scale 1:10,000

Floor plans · sections
scale 1.1,500

1 Parking lot
2 Main site entrance
3 Administration building
4 Employee restaurant,
  "Stripes"
  (Architects: Kauffmann
  Theilig & Partner)
5 Adi Dassler track & field
6 Adi Dassler Brand Center
7 Convention hotel
8 Sports center (planned)
9 "Arena" with projection
  surface
10 Bar
11 Catering
12 Assembly
13 Atrium
14 Office
15 Forum
16 "Walk of fame"
  exhibition
17 Storage
18 Delivery/parking
19 "Working area": collection
20 "Working area": design
  concepts retail
21 Information/entrance
22 Void
23 Seating, arena
24 Audio/video room
25 Adi Dassler VIP room
26 HVAC control room

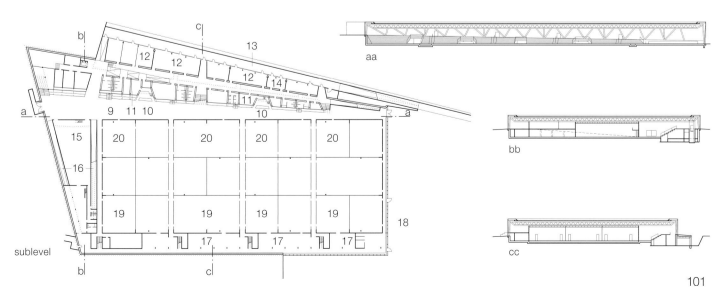

sublevel

aa

bb

cc

101

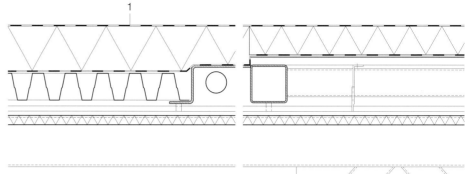

Vertical section   scale 1:20

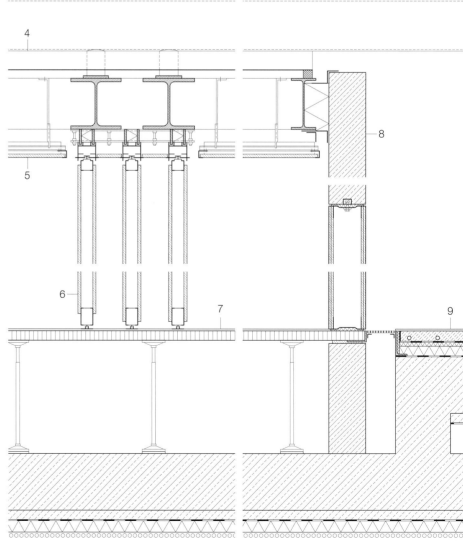

1 plastic roofing membrane, mineral wool
  insulation 130–230 mm, vapor barrier,
  steel metal decking 150 mm, acoustic fleece
2 top and bottom chord, steel hollow profile
  Ø 273/10/8 mm
3 diagonal member, steel hollow profile
  Ø 159/8 mm
4 metal decking 100 mm
5 acoustic ceiling tile, mineral fiber 19 mm
6 light sliding wall, standard position:
  gypsum board, melamine coating 12.5 mm
  framing, aluminum 75 mm
  gypsum board, melamine coating 12.5 mm
7 rubber coating, press board 50 mm,
  void with pedestals 600 mm, waterproof
  concrete 300 mm, base layer 50 mm,
  separation layer PE foil, extruded polystyrol
  insulation 60 mm, crushed gravel 200 mm
8 prefabricated reinforced concrete soffit
  200 mm, steel sheet metal painted finish 2 mm,
  gypsum board 2× 12.5 mm, framing 150 mm,
  gypsum board 2× 12.5 mm
9 hard aggregate screed, polyurethane
  coating, underfloor heating system 55 mm,
  PE foil separation layer, mineral wool insulation 70 mm, vapor barrier, waterproof concrete 300 mm, base layer 50 mm, PE foil
  separation layer, crushed gravel 200 mm
10 shock absorbers, hydraulic facade/roof
  separation
11 movable HEA steel profile 180 mm
12 laminate glass black tinted 2× 8 mm,
  airspace 16 mm, security glass 6 mm,
  steel profile ⌴ 75/70 mm, laminate glass
  flange 3× 12 mm
13 main column, diagonal steel hollow profile
  Ø 273/10 mm
14 coarse aggregate concrete stucco 30 mm,
  cast-in-place concrete wall 300 mm, framing
  aluminum 75 mm, gypsum board 2× 12.5 mm

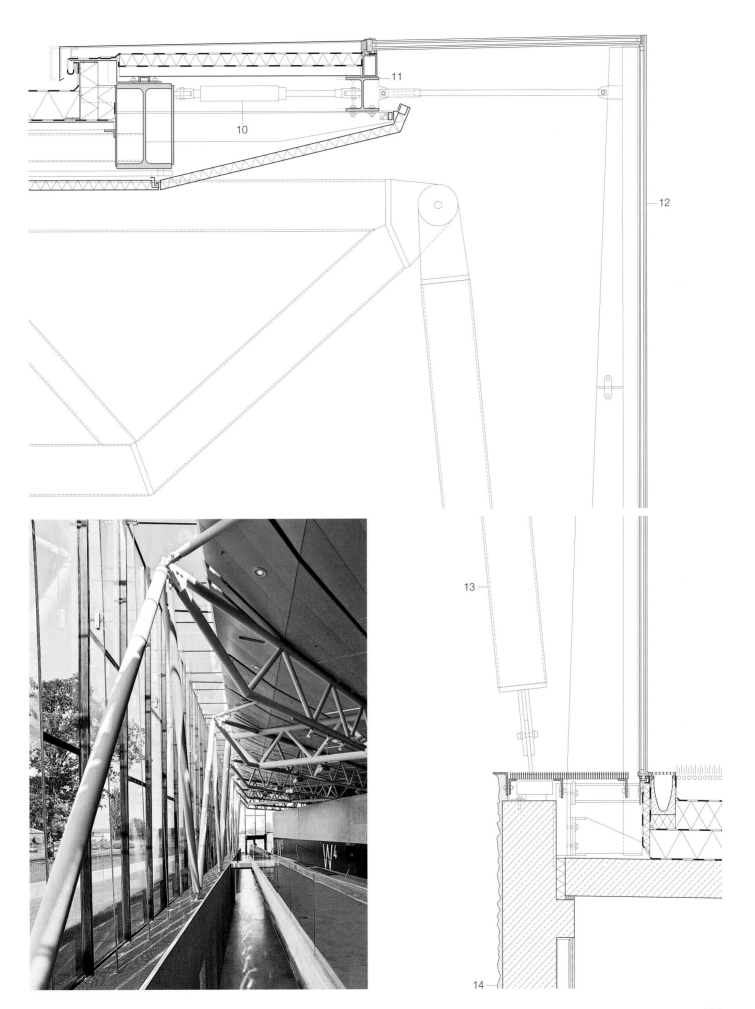

10

11

12

13

14

Baufritz exhibition building in Erkheim

Architects: a.ml und partner, Nuremberg

Four "style environments" are presented by the "home-makers" of theis manufacturer of houses based on wood construction, serving to aid potential clients in making their decisions.

Driving along the highway from Munich to Lindau, drivers pass the new exhibition building of the Baufritz corporation, manufacturers of wood residential houses based on ecologically sound construction methods. The one-story building, gently floating above the landscape, is intended as exhibition and presentation building and serves for information as well as presentation of construction components, materials, and spatial situations.

Movement as design principle
The site of the new building, located directly next to the highway, inspired the architects to conceptualize movement and change and adeptly incorporate these topics into the design by use of simple means. They arranged six demonstration facades along the facade facing the highway, scenographically placed within large-format, funnel-shaped frames, perceived by drivers passing by as images. The two long facades are completely without openings; only the placement of interior courtyards can be recognized in the facade design. The facade consists of vertical, free-standing wood louvers that are mounted in front of a prefabricated wood wall, printed with a pattern of rhomboid shapes. Observers' movements create visual interference patterns that result in the impression of a continuously changing structure, even though the structure is actually rigid and immovable. Depending on speed of movement, the geometrical pattern changes. Also, the corporate

logo, placed on the longitudinal facades, can only be recognized when in motion. As soon as someone approaches the building, it dissolves into a pattern of stripes and vanishes. Only the short southern facade is completely glazed. Here, a gracious plaza welcomes visitors.

Residential examples, 1:1 scale
Within the interior, the individual use areas are spatially structured by topically designed interior courtyards. In addition, the atriums provide for sufficient daylight intake in the interior with its intentionally introverted character. Across a total area of approximately 1,800 m², four different styles (emotion, values, sensuality, and knowledge) are presented to customers in order to help them decide on their future home. The future clients can look at, walk through, and use the most diverse selection of entrances, completely furnished children's rooms, living rooms or bathrooms in 1:1 scale. Within the "tour of senses", visitors can finally actively and sensually feel the numerous qualities of wood as building material. Color, sound, touch, and smell of wood can be experienced here within architecture. The five interior courtyards provide a special experience in this context: Three small, topically designed atriums covered with a pergola along the western facade accompany visitors on their way to the demonstration spaces. Two small and deep interior courtyards are located along the eastern facade. The "Japanese" courtyard is clad in delicate larch wood louvers on all sides. Gravel-covered floors and pine bonsai provide a Far-Eastern atmosphere. The fifth interior courtyard, the only one that visitors can enter, connects architecture and nature through its glazed facade. The noise of the heavily frequented highway is no longer audible here.

Site plan
scale 1:2,000

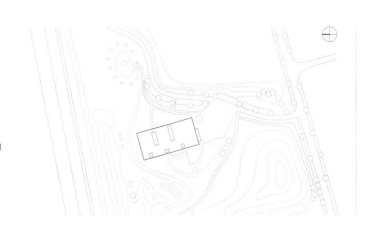

Project data:

Use:	exhibition and retail building
Construction:	wood frame
Clear room height:	3.25 m
Gross volume:	9,054 m³
Gross footprint:	1,810 m²
Exhibition area:	900 m²
Completion:	2005
Construction time:	8 months

Elevations · sections · floor plan
scale 1:500

1 Foyer
2 Reception
3 Office
4 Espresso bar
5 Shop
6 Kitchen
7 Wardrobe

8 Interior courtyard
9 Tour of senses
10 Japanese interior courtyard
11 Conference rooms
12 Exhibition area
13 Relaxation room
14 Exhibition, "values"
15 Exhibition, "sensuality"
16 Exhibition, "knowledge"
17 Exhibition, "emotion"

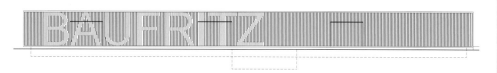

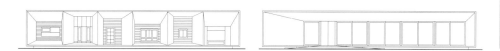

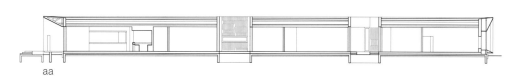

aa

bb

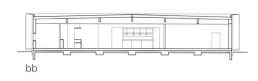

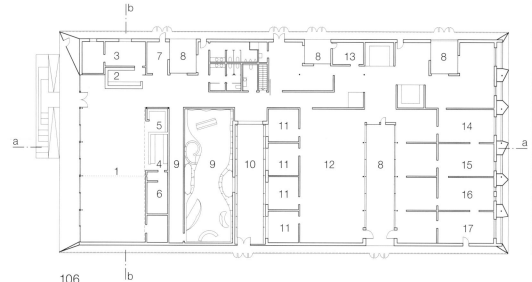

Floor plans
scale 1:200

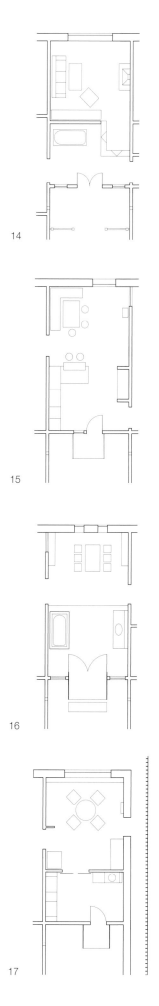

14

15

16

17

Proper light for presentations

Thomas Schielke

1

Ideal lighting concepts are indispensable for successful presentations in retail spaces, at trade shows, or at exhibitions. These concepts are based on professional lighting design for creating a specific spatial atmosphere by using appropriate lamps, light fixtures, and light control systems, but also for directing the attention of the observer towards defined targets.

The eye perceives an object through light. As result, light determines how an observer sees an object, and even if it is regarded as worth viewing. This is especially the case for objects on display for retail. Here, the viewer is exposed to various competing visual impressions. This is why light plays a decisive role in the design of product presentations, whether in retail spaces, display windows, or exhibition stands. Well planned lighting draws attention, makes items visible in an ideal way, and serves for orientation and wellbeing of viewers. When properly designed, lighting can give a business an unmistakable character, transform an exhibition stand into a center of gravity, and turn window shopping and buying things into a real experience.

One major functional aspect of lighting design is the creation of hierarchies of perception that enable spatial organization. Equally important is the use of light for creating moods. Modern lighting and control technology serves to seamlessy integrate both functions and develop sophisticated lighting concepts for creating lighting scenes for various lighting tasks.

The terminology defined by the American lighting designer Richard Kelly has proven useful for the communication between lighting designer and client, as well as for analysis of architectural lighting. General illumination that basically enables visual perception is described as "ambient luminescence". "Focal glow" creates hierarchies of perception by use of contrasts in luminosity and lighting accents. It both directs the viewers' gaze to spatial zones or objects and supports their orientation. The "play of brilliants" includes lighting effects that are used for atmospheric or decorative purposes – for instance a lighting object or colored light that influences the color temperature of a space. Lighting concepts are successful when they combine all three of these components in a balanced relationship.

Lighting concepts for corporate design
Corporate lighting concepts strenghten a brand's corporate design with a characteristic lighting concept. Successful corporate design is based on two principles: on the one hand the development of lighting moods that correspond to a brand, on the other hand the selection of light fixtures that already convey a particular brand character in their design. Recessed ceiling light fixtures, e.g. downlights, are a way to elegantly integrate lighting technology into architecture. Alternatively, additive lighting systems such as trackmount spotlights or pendant lamps have an expressive character, displaying technical details in addition to their illuminating effect. The selection of a particular light fixture design appropriate for a corporate image or a brand may seem simple in comparison. The creation of a characteristic lighting atmosphere however demands analyzing how both light and brand are perceived.

Light and atmosphere
Illumination not only supports perception and orientation, it can also provoke emotional responses and communicate an aesthetic value. A strong atmospheric unity is created when illumination corresponds to brand, space, and material. Targeted dramatized illumination before a dark background e. g. can emphasize the exclusive quality of a product. Strong contrasts and colors increase emotional qualities. The perception of luminosity influences the first overall impression of a space: An illuminated room suggests spatiousness and creates an association to daytime, whereas dark spaces provide the mysterious backdrop for theatrical dramatizations. A basic illumination with diffuse light, e.g. with indirect illumination or light ceilings, gives spaces a soft, calm, and neutral character. On the other hand, directed light e.g. with accent lighting created by spotlights provides intensive modeling with strong contrasts of light and shadow. The selection of light colors from warm white to daylight white subtly influences color temperature. The impression created by colored light via color filter or RGB color mixture is more direct; not only does it draw attention, but it also creates an unmistakable ambience when used across surfaces. Dynamic light with different scenes for day and evening, for special events or decopoints offers a broad range of individual lighting solutions and produces a vivid image. The use of colorful light for creating background lighting corresponds to the desire for a matching atmosphere. On the other hand, frontal accent illumination with white light enables very good color reproduction quality and emphasizes product characteristics such as material and color in an ideal way.

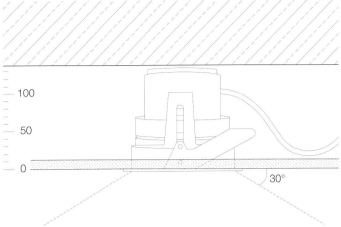

2

3

Zoning of retail spaces

A lighting concept also needs to take the subdivision of retail spaces into different zones into account. Lighting sources should not dominate spaces so items can remain in the focus of attention. Contrasts in illuminance organize the space, define zones, and separate important things from less important ones by hierarchies of perception. In order to effectively contrast with products on display, aisles should receive less lighting than the actual merchandise areas. For sales areas, the proper relation between general and accent illumination is crucial. Sufficient horizontal and vertical illuminance provide for homogeneous illumination of goods.

Spotlights accentuate particular objects and decopoints. A contrast ratio of 1:10 with ambient lighting is necessary to achieve a visible difference. Vertical inclination of 30° of spotlights leads to a balanced modeling of products. It makes objects appear three-dimensional and avoids strong drop shadows. Scattered light and incorrectly aligned light fixtures can reduce light quality through glare. Direct glare by spotlights is avoided when their vertical inclination does not exceed 30°. Projections and image vignettes (gobos) provide items with expressive light patterns.

Illuminating architectural elements such as vaulted ceilings or columns emphasizes the character of a space. Illuminated walls define a space and can also provide accentuation of shelving and items. Wall washers are an optional vertical illumination source and provide a very homogeneous luminosity from floor to ceiling. Glancing light directly along walls emphasizes textures. Walls backlit with colored light can serve as backdrop for a dynamic product dramatization.

Open stage for the exhibition appearance

At exhibitions, corporate exhibition stands, often belonging to the same type of business, compete with one another for the attention of visitors within a limited amount of space. Aside from the architecture of the exhibition stand and decorative elements, most of all lighting serves to draw attention. The greatest degree of attention is created by scenographic lighting effects, with which visitors of theaters, stage shows, and other events are familiar.

Scenographic light integrates dimensions of space and time into lighting design. A number of instruments is available for this purpose: digitally dimmable washers, LED-spotlights with RGB color mixture, projectors with gobo rotator – and related control systems that both integrate dramatizing effects with every-day illumination in a unified system and make them comfortably accessible.

4

1 The brilliant light of spotlights dramatizes the display window. Dramatized lighting effects are created with lighting technology used in theaters. These are complemented by the chandelier as a "light to look at".
2 The possibilities of dramatization of window displays through lighting reach from a concentrated focus on displayed items to a mysterious play of bright lights.
3 Ease of assembly and compact dimensions of downlights can have a positive effect on the overall cost efficiency of a contruction project. A cut-off angle of 30° guarantees good visual comfort.
4 Spotlights and tracks characterize this interior space. The glass elements and the metallic glittering surfaces create a sophisticated play of reflection and transparency.

5

These concepts for exhibition lighting cause two worlds of lighting to collide: on the one hand, the light fixtures and control systems of architectural lighting, on the other the lighting tools of the stage, used for event-oriented and theatrical illumination. Architectural light fixtures embody high demands for design and can provide an exhibition stand with important detailing. Opposed to this, the lighting tools used for the stage, e. g. moveable multifunctional floodlights for effect-oriented lighting, often have a rather technical appearance. In the theater, they are invisible to the viewers, thus they don't need to meet aesthetic demands. At exhibition stands however, many stage lights can be seen, resulting in a technical visual appearance.

In professions such as film, advertisement, or scenography, using storyboards for designing scenes is a long established practice. They permit illustration of a sequence of changing perspectives and subjects. As a tool for design of scenographic lighting, they can serve as a creative script for the spatial and temporal succession of lighting dramatization. Sketches serve to illustrate e. g. dynamics of luminosity, contrast conditions, light colors, and lighting effects.

Light fixtures made-to-order
The decision for one particular type of light fixture depends on criteria defined by the intended lighting impressions and the framework conditions of the project. For instance, the light color of a light fixture influences the quality of colors of illuminated objects. Warm white light colors emphasize warm colors, e. g. red and yellow, whereas daylight white light colors underscore cold colors such as blue and green. The quality of a light fixture is determined by color reproduction and color stability throughout its entire lifespan.

Based on thermal light emission, halogen incandescent light fixtures generate dimmable warm white light. Their continuous spectrum provides for very good color reproduction, and their compact form enables both directing light in an ideal way and attaining a brilliant lighting effect. Low voltage halogen reflector light fixtures with cold light mirror contain only a very low degree of infrared light in their light cone and result in minimizing thermal loads in illuminated objects. They are available in different types of small angle scattering.

6

Fluorescent light fixtures are characterized by a high light output and lifespan. The light colors of this dimmable light fixture type are warm, neutral, or daylight white. Types are available including fluorescent strip lighting and compact fluorescent light fixtures with a diffuse lighting impression. They are suitable for a homogeneous and cost-efficient basic illumination.

High intensity discharge lamps have an excellent light output, high luminous flux rates, long lifespan, and good color reproduction. Modern ceramic metal halide lamps feature good color stability and reproduction as well as integrated UV-protection. Metal halide lamps provide a 9000 hour lifespan with a light output of up to 90 lm/W, a significantly higher efficiency than conventional incandescent halogen lamps with a lifespan of 2000 hours at 20 lm/W.

7

LEDs have a very long lifespan and small size. When using LEDs with different colors, the light color can be adjusted non-parametrically via RGB-color mixture. LEDs are also available in warm white and daylight white and constitute an alternative to low voltage halogen lamps.

Specialists for different lighting purposes
Flexible light fixtures such as trackmount spotlights are ideal for illuminating retail and presentation spaces. They are used for accent lighting with different lighting inclinations and can be combined with a variety of accessories. The place of installation and alignment can be adapted according to changing presentation demands. Contour spotlights enable the creation of different light cone contours or lighting patterns for decorative effects by image vignette projection.

Special accessories for unique demands in accent lighting are available for many light fixture types. Sculpture lenses configure round light cones into elliptical forms in order to more evenly illuminate objects with long shapes such as mannequins. Flood lenses widen the light cone and create softer borders. Glass interference color filters are characterized by exactly defined and delimited colors. Ultraviolet and infrared filters protect objects from harmful radiation. Honeycomb grids or glare shields increase visual comfort. Correction filters change the light color in a subtle way, and skin tone filters improve the impression of natural, warm colors.

Floodlights comprise a further group of track-mount light fixtures. They distribute light in a broad beam with a soft gradient for illuminating product groups or background areas. Wallwashers however, with their asymmetric light distribution, only create light useful for vertical surfaces. The result is a high degree of uniformity of illuminance across wall surfaces.

The range of recessed ceiling light fixtures reaches from classic downlights with broad, symmetrical light distribution for general illumination, to downlight wallwashers and lens wallwashers for vertical illumination, to adjustable spotlights for flexible accent lighting. An optimized reflector technology guarantees a high efficiency of lighting. The dimming angle reduces glare and thus improves visual comfort.

Flexibility with intelligent light control
With digital light control, lighting is quickly and simply adjustable to different requirements both during installation as well as operation. For instance, specific lighting scenes can be defined depending on daylight conditions. Through sensors, light control reacts automatically to daylight and can efficiently adjust sun protection in combination with interior lighting. Differentiated adjustment of illuminance is indispensable for a high-profile lighting design in presentation areas. The programming of dynamic light with stage-like lighting effects increases the intensity of customers' experiences and draws more attention.
DALI or digital addressable lighting interface constitutes the digital standard in lighting technology for architecture and serves for controlling lighting within spaces, for instance in a store or an exhibition. The system features separate control and power lines, and operational units are addressed individually. Thus, the creation of lighting groups, spatial zones, or lighting scenes does not occur on the level of wiring but via the software of the DALI-system. Interfaces enable integration of DALI into a superordinate building utility control system. Thus, digital lighting control offers a high degree of flexibility in lighting design and in every-day operations.

5 Lens wall washers with metal halide lamps create homogeneous illumination and improve the appearance of fabric colors.
6 The goal of dramatized lighting concepts for trade shows is to draw the attention of customers. Scenographic lighting with dynamic lighting sequences offers continuously changing impressions.
7 The secret of dynamic, colorful lighting installations in the background and an optimum light reflection in the foreground consists of an additional accent illumination for the mannequins in the window display.
8 The combination of wall washers and recessed spotlights offers vertical illumination for walls and shelves, but also flexible accent lighting for tables, clothes racks, and mannequins.

8

"Freudenhaus" optician store in Munich

Architects: AIGNER ARCHITECTURE, Munich

Sections
Floor plan
scale 1:200

1 Entrance
2 Sales floor
3 Counter
4 Cash register
5 Restroom
6 Refraction
7 Storage

Futuristic tubes, serving for dramatic presentation of eyewear, are the "eyecatcher" in this stylish shop.

The Freudenhaus Eyewear label, operating numerous branch stores in Munich, intended to adapt its existing corporate architecture to a young, trendy target group and simultaneously ensure continuity of the existing corporate identity. For the only 50 m² of sales floor area, the architects developed a concept that awakens the curiosity of the young target group and, at the same time, leaves center stage to eyewear, by use of a minimalist design gesture and clear design.

Porthole storefront

The small retail space, which housed a shoe store prior to remodeling, is located in the Schwabing quarter of the city of Munich. From outside, the storefront with its offbeat design, in which videos featuring the current line of eyewear models are projected onto the round porthole apertures, obstructs the view to what is hidden behind the great metal door. In the interior, the interweaving of color, shapes, and lighting creates a calm, clear atmosphere and thus emphasizes the brand image.

Purist interior design

With the white, even surfaces from floor to ceiling, the store serves as a neutral background for the integrated presentation elements.

The eyewear items on display are arranged along the wall within porthole merchandise fixtures – the characteristic brand sign. The glass shelving is indirectly lit by fluorescent light fixtures mount behind the backdrop wall. More memorable however are the tubes protruding from wall and ceiling. By use of counterweights, the tubes can be extended and retracted as required in order to prevent direct access to the eyewear items. The 16 tubes are made of transparent or satinized acrylic glass and indirectly lit by LEDs.

The defining element of the sales floor however is the central, long, cantilevered sales counter. This spatial sculpture is supported by a steel structure and clad in solid surface material. It offers plenty of storage with integrated drawers and, at the same time, comprises an exhibition object. The rear section includes refraction and storage.

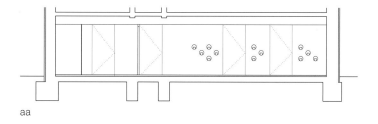

aa

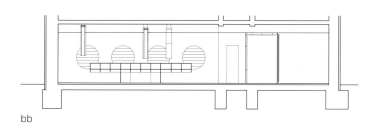

bb

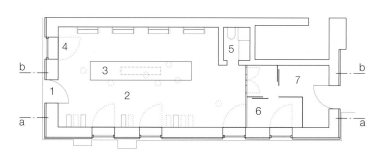

Project Data:

Use:	retail/commercial
Construction:	masonry, reinforced concrete ceiling
Clear room height:	2.59 m
Gross volume:	179.74 m³
Gross footprint:	69.13 m²
Sales floor area:	50.68 m²
Total cost:	€ 98,000 (gross)
Completion:	2008
Construction time:	2 months

Vertical sections · horizontal sections
ceiling and wall tubes
scale 1:10

1 suspended ceiling,
  gypsum board 12.5 mm
2 acrylic glass casing, transparent
  ∅ 300 mm / 8 mm
3 guide track, aluminum profile
  ⊔ 40/20 mm
4 aluminum cover ring
  ∅ 200 mm / 5 mm
5 LED indirect light

6 acrylic glass,
  satinized white 10 mm
7 wall construction:
  wood composite panel,
  white paint finish 18 mm
  counter battens
  existing masonry wall 320 mm
8 acrylic glass merchandise shelving,
  satinized white 10 mm
9 canted edge, sheet aluminum,
  powder coated white 10 mm
10 acrylic glass pegs, transparent
  ∅ 5 mm / 50 mm

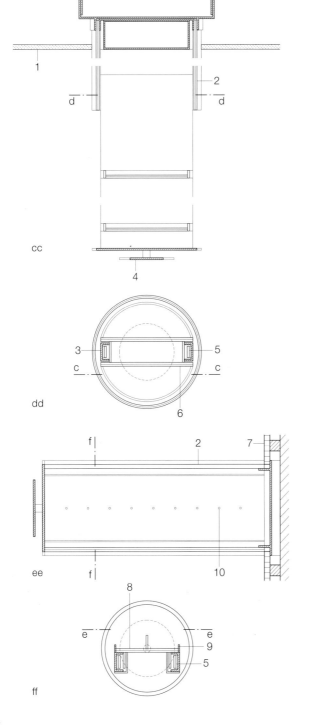

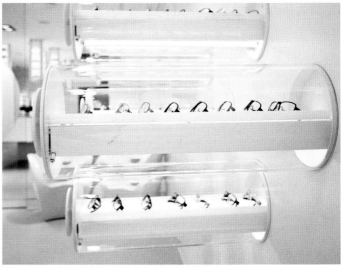

Whiteleys Shopping Center in London

Architects: Lifschutz Davidson Sandilands, London

Project Data:

Use:	retail/commercial
Construction:	steel
Clear room height:	2.6–4.3 m (atrium heights: 9–25 m)
Gross volume:	25,000 m³ (including atriums)
Gross footprint:	2,700 m²
Sales floor area:	580 m²
Total cost:	€ 1.10 million (gross)
Completion:	2008
Construction time:	3 months

An open markeet hall with wine and delicatessen counters and stylish design was created in the historic context of Whiteleys, which opened as a traditional department store in 1912.

Whiteleys shopping center is located in Bayswater in immediate proximity to Hyde Park and is considered one of London's most important department stores. The neoclassical building, erected in 1912, is subject to historic preservation and features an impressive, expansive atrium with glass dome and cast iron stair construction.

The new delicatessen area is designed as an open "market hall" and is situated on the ground floor along the central building axes. The architects developed a flexible design vocabulary that would, on the one hand, enable adapting to specific spatial, technological, and branding related demands, while on the other hand being capable of representing a strong, unified corporate identity. The presentation system was also intended to have a modern, fresh, and unique appearance that reflected the style of the operator, Food Inc., and at the same time adapted to its surrounding within the historical building in a harmonic way.

Presentation systems

The desire for simple forms and materials led to the development of a three-dimensional band structure intended to visually connect the diverse departments across the entire length of the sales floor. The endless silvery band thus serves as a border for merchandise fixtures. The continuously repetitive reference heights of sales counters and shelving also provide for a unified appearance throughout all departments.

Material and color selections

Polished stainless steel, white solid surface material, and glass comprise, on the one hand, a calm background for the extensive product range and offer, on the other hand, an elegant and cost-efficient solution. The materials also need to meet demands in regard to scratch proofing, fireproofing, and hygiene. The restrained color selection of white and grey also contributes to the unified appearance. The construction consists of steel hollow profiles clad in MDF sheathing covered with stainless steel sheet metal or solid surface panels.

Floor plan
scale 1:3,000

1 Main entrance
2 Juice bar
3 Seafood counter
4 Meat counter
5 Delicatessen
6 Cafeteria
7 Grocery department
8 Wine shop
9 Cheese counter
10 Bakery and patisserie
11 Ice cream counter

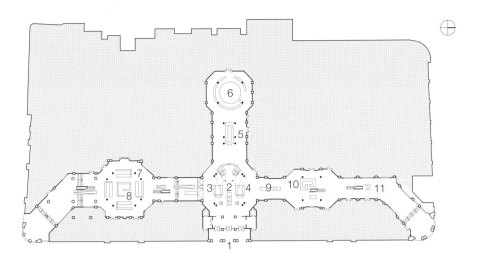

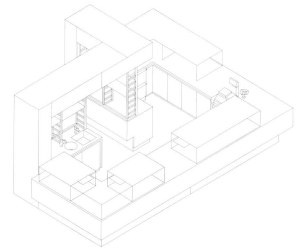

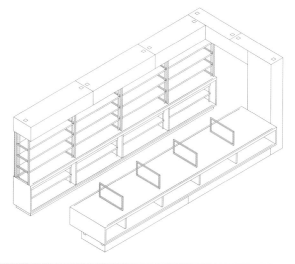

12 MDF 12 mm substrate panel covered
with stainless steel panel 1 mm
13 indirect fluorescent lighting
14 framing steel pipe
profile ⊘ 30/30/1.2 mm
15 cross bracing steel pipe
⊘ 25/25/1.2 mm
16 rear panel toughened glass 20 mm
17 shelving system, chrome plated
18 solid surface material 12 mm
19 slots for price tags
20 framing steel pipe ⊘ 30/30/1.2 mm
21 adjustable toughened glass panel 10 mm
22 rear panel toughened glass 10 mm
23 showcase toughened glass 10 mm,
UV-proof

Food shelving
Delicatessen counter
Isometric illustrations
Vertical sections   scale 1:20

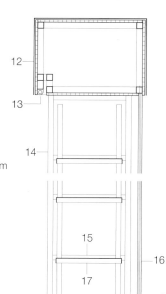

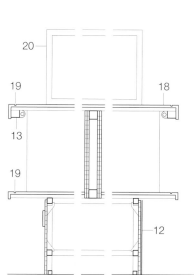

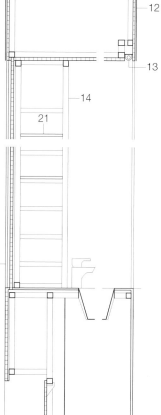

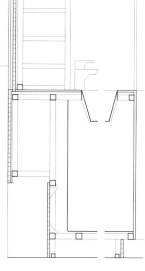

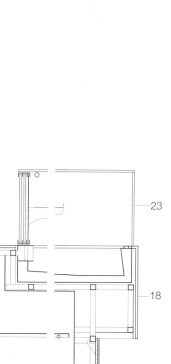

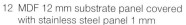

117

MPREIS Supermarket in Innsbruck

Architects: Rainer Köberl, Innsbruck

The mirrored ceiling and artificial light wells provide for varied plays of light and an unusual shopping experience

The MPREIS corporation has gained a reputation with its high-quality supermarkets in the landscape of Tyrol in Austria. For the lower level of the Innsbruck train station, the supermarket chain required an innovative spatial solution for a store without a landscape and without natural illumination, in a 60 m long and only 3.10 m high space.

Lighting concept

The difficult basic conditions led to a solution that was defined by the lighting concept. Artificial light wells, comprised of suspended ceiling segments made of white plastic laminate louvers with fluorescent lighting strips mount above them, signal the presence of the entrance and checkout area below, as well as two perimeter areas with delicatessen counters. These light wells contrast with other areas in which a ceiling made of black enameled float glass reflects the space below in a fascinating way. A bistro area is located in the front area of the store. Orange lighting cubes are suspended above a wooden counter. Above the center of the counter, a transition between the light ceiling and the black float glass occurs.

Elegant atmosphere

The merchandise is precisely lit by specially developed lighting fixtures that illuminate the space through reflections. Thus, additional general illumination is not required. The colors and shapes of each individual product group are reflected by the glass ceiling. Thus, a calm ambience is created in the subterranean, rather difficult space in a very unique way; creating an elegant, metropolitan shopping experience. The bordeaux red poured synthetic resin flooring dampens loud noise made by shopping carts and also improves the acoustic quality of the space.

Project Data:

Use:	retail/commercial
Construction:	reinforced concrete, glass
Clear room height:	3.10 m
Gross volume:	5,015 m³
Gross usable area:	1,135 m²
Sales floor area:	992 m²
Total cost:	€ 839,600
Completion:	2004
Construction time:	4 months

Section   scale 1:250
Floor plan   scale 1:750

1 Bistro area
2 Counters
3 Refrigerated shelving
4 Produce
5 Delicatessen counters
6 Tea kitchen
7 Employee room
8 Employee entrance
9 Storage

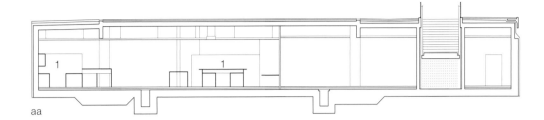

aa

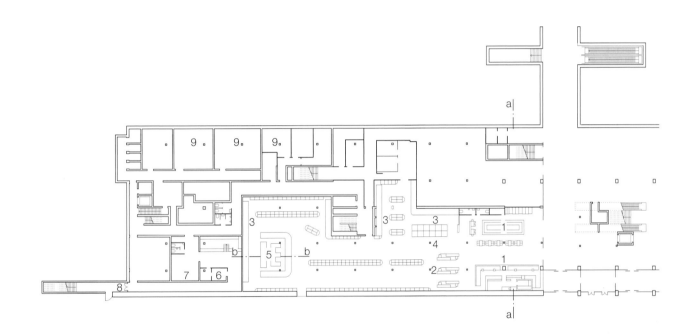

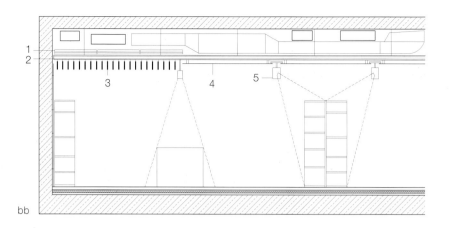

bb

Section
scale 1:100
Vertical sections suspended glass ceiling
scale 1:5

1 fluorescent lighting strip
2 steel profile ⊔ 120, perforated sheet metal,
  spot-welded to ⊔-profile
3 plastic laminate louver, white 19/200 mm,
  suspended from perforated sheet metal,
  at 150 mm o.c.
4 laminated glass, enameled black 2× 6 mm
5 spotlight
6 concrete anchor M16
7 connector nut
8 threaded rod M12
9 steel profile ⊔ 120
10 counter nut
11 anchored track 74/48/5 mm
12 aluminum profile 20/50 mm
13 polyurethan foam tape, self-adhesive
14 bolt connection

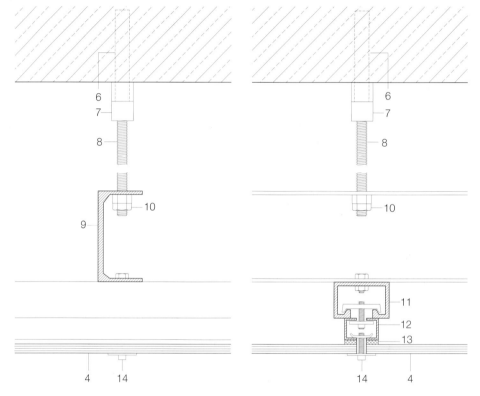

Edeka Supermarket in Ingolstadt

Architects: ATP Architekten und Ingenieure, Munich

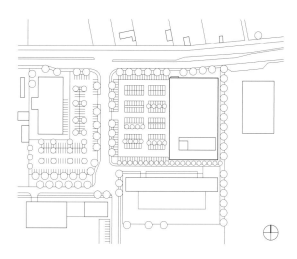

The standardized modules of the new Corporate Architecture concept for a trade chain provide for a consistent appearance.

Until now, exterior visual appearance had been a rather low priority for many super market chains. Edeka however developed new concepts intended to meet consumer demands and at the same time win new customers and contribute to an increase of profits. Opposed to the MPREIS-chain stores in the Austrian region of Tyrol with their individual floor plan concepts and exterior visual appearance, the trade chain aimed at creating a series of standardized modules that could lead to a systemizing of separate individual stores.

The new principles of Edeka's Corporate Architecture are presence, transparency, orientation, and clarity. An urban design directive was formulated that called for placing building volumes immediately next to streets and thus attract the attention of people walking by. The stores are intended to contribute to improving the quality of mostly peripheral environments by creating a qualified, significant architectural presence. Completely glazed facades oriented towards streets or parking lots create transparency and openness. Targeted views of the interior showing the activity within the store and particular item selections are thus possible. The visual impression of openness created by the exterior is continued into the interior by an unobstructed entrance and exit as well as the only 1.60 m tall merchandise shelving. Customers thus receive an overview of the product range and can orient themselves in a better way.

In all Edeka chain stores, the aim is to provide a special feature in the future as well: the Corporate Identity Supersign.

Special functions such as vestibule, café, bakery shop, and shopping cart bays in the parking lot are placed within back-lit yellow containers.

Modularly constructed pavilion

The first prototype of this new Corporate Architecture concept is located in the east of Ingolstadt. The building geometry consists of slab-shaped and rectangular elements; its design is reminiscent of a simple pavilion. The purist cube shape receives added complexity by the integrated entrance container including café and bakery shop as well as the cantilevered roof along the parking lot, thus responding to the urban design context. Barrier-free access and the continuous, charcoal-colored flooring create seamless transitions from exterior to interior.

Interior and product range

The sales floor area of about 2,700 m² is organized on the ground level along a 6 × 8 m grid and designed as open market place. The restrained material selection of floors, shelving, ceilings, and steel columns creates a pleasant atmosphere. The entire market can be overviewed due to the functional, low shelving. Individual departments of the market, e.g. produce or wine selection, are specially marked by additional integrated components or different material selections. Cosmetics departments as well are accentuated by use of curved shelving with illuminated glass shelves. The artificial illumination is oriented on the structure of the shelving. Recessed ceiling downlights provide homogeneous interior illumination.

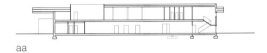

aa

bb

Site plan
scale 1:4,000
Sections · floor plans
scale 1:1,000

1 Entry plaza
2 Vestibule
3 Cafeteria
4 Bakery shop
5 Checkout

6 Produce
7 Cosmetics
8 Low temperature
   cooling
9 Meat/sausages
10 Store management
11 Storage
12 Delivery
13 Employee rooms
14 Utilities

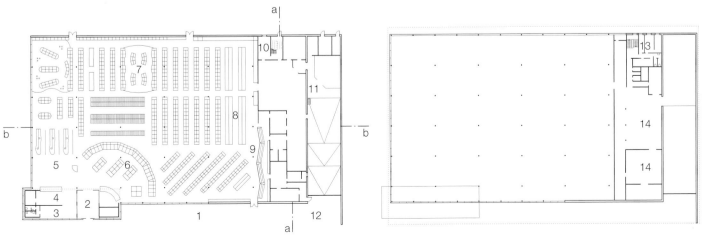

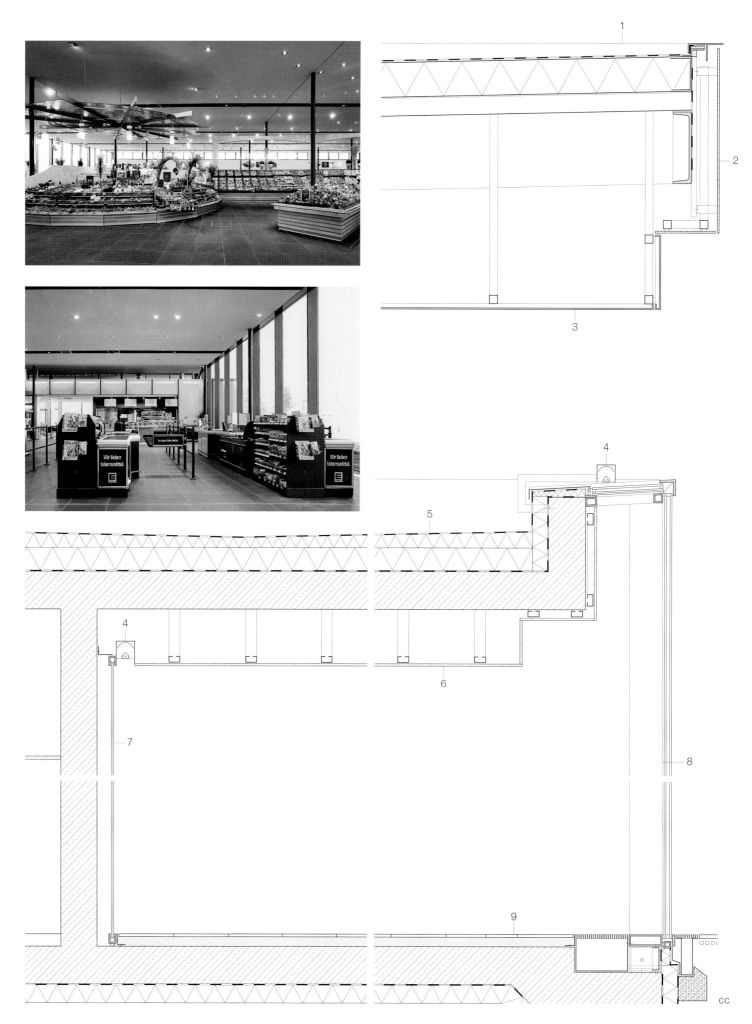

Vertical section   scale 1:20
Floor plan • sections   scale 1:200

1 roof construction:
   plastic roofing membrane 3 mm
   insulation 18 mm
   vapor barrier
   canted steel sheet metal 15 mm
   metal decking 80 mm, steel profile 380/20 mm
2 fiber-cement panel 2,660/980 mm
3 aluminum composite panel 2,660/1,730 mm
4 lighting profile, fluorescent material
5 plastic roofing membrane 3 mm
   insulation, in the slope 180 mm
   insulation 200 mm, vapor barrier,
   reinforced concrete 250 mm
6 suspended ceiling, gypsum board 12.5 mm
7 laminate glass 15 mm
   steel profile ⊔ 30/50 mm
8 curtain wall façade 180/60 mm
9 floor construction:
   stoneware tile 15 mm, thick bed mortar
   50 mm, reinforced concrete 200 mm

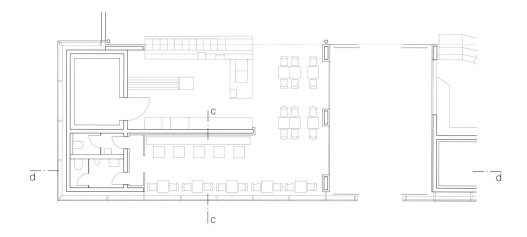

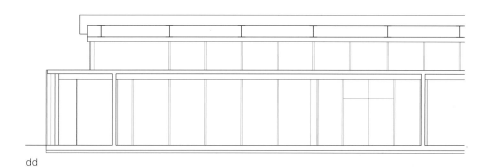

Project data:

Use:	retail/commercial
Construction:	steel
Clear room height:	4.5 m
Gross volume:	30,000 m³
Gross story area:	4,400 m²
Useable area:	3,640 m²
Total cost:	€ 3.132 million (gross)
Completion:	2006
Construction time:	6 months

Noise barrier with integrated car showroom near Utrecht

Architects: ONL [Oosterhuis_Lénárd], Rotterdam

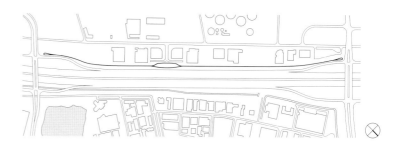

The structure of a noise barrier merges into a glass shell which is being used as an impressive showroom by a car retailer.

A special architectural highlight is presented to drivers passing by along the A2 near Utrecht: The architects integrated a car showroom within a noise barrier, 1.5 km long and separating the highway from a commercial area. Accordingly, its form was inspired by the motif of dynamic automobile design shapes. The showroom interior can be viewed from the highway which runs at a distance of merely 15 m. Here, covering about 5,000 m² showroom area, luxury cars are available for purchase. Shop and garage in the lowest level are set back. Here, only the roofs of cars and the heads of the mechanics working on them can be seen.

Dynamic shell

The noise barrier expands dramatically in its middle, becoming the "cockpit" of the car showroom, seamlessly integrated into its curvaceous design. Accordingly, the triangular glazing elements become larger and larger, doubling in size towards the center. The insulation glazing with a thickness of 42 mm is mount directly onto the extremely stiff structural steel construction. The selected glazing is equipped with sun protection coating, the strength of which increases from the base of the building to its roofline. This enables a clear view of the exhibited cars in the lower area, while providing sun protection in the upper area. As opposed to the glazed display façade, the rear façade of the building, clad in sheet metal, is almost completely windowless.

Interior showroom design

Beneath the arched glass skin, the spacious showroom interior offers an abundance of free space for the presentation of various luxury car brands. Very broad, gently sloped ramps also serve as exhibition areas and create a dynamic succession of spaces. Sales counters are comprised of freely placed semi-circular furniture. In order to provide a good acoustic quality of space, despite the hard surfaces of the glass façade, the ceiling surfaces are covered with a sound-proofing fabric. Suspended spotlights along the roofline and downlights provide for appropriate illumination of cars.

Noise barrier construction

In order to keep the number of foundation piles for the noise barrier as low as possible, a space frame spans 9 m from pier to pier. Security glass with 6 mm thickness is mount directly onto the space frame consisting of hollow steel profiles. The glazing is framed in hard rubber profiles and panels overlap similar to a reptile's scales. Thus, the individual glass panes can slide past each other in the case of temperature related expansion and contraction of the structure.

Project Data:

Use:	car dealership/commercial
Construction:	steel
Clear room height:	4–11 m
Gross volume:	35,000 m³
Gross footprint:	6,400 m²
Exhibition area:	5,000 m²
Total cost:	€ 5.5 million
Completion:	2005
Construction time:	11 months

aa

Site plan
scale 1:15,000
Section · floor plans
scale 1:1,500

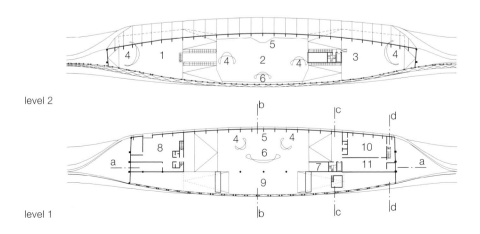

level 2

level 1

1 Exhibition Lamborghini
2 Exhibition Bentley
3 Exhibition Rolls Royce
4 Sales office
5 Coffee bar
6 Lounge
7 Car elevator
8 Utilities
9 Exhibition Maserati
10 Office
11 Break room

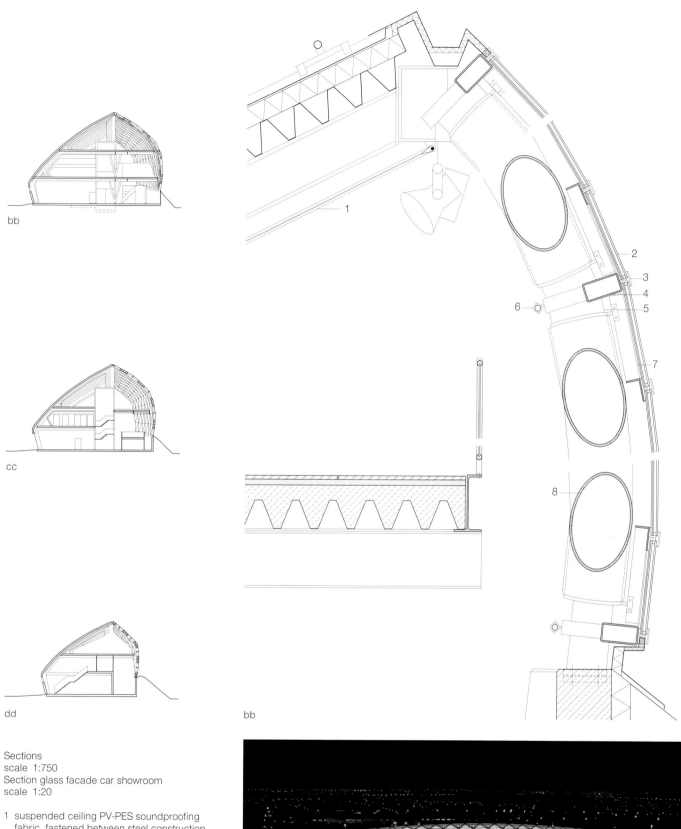

bb

cc

dd

bb

Sections
scale 1:750
Section glass facade car showroom
scale 1:20

1 suspended ceiling PV-PES soundproofing fabric, fastened between steel construction members
2 sun protection float glass 10 mm + air space 15 mm + laminate glass 17 mm, black caulking butt joints
3 glass fastener, stainless steel, black
4 steel pipe ⊏⊐ 200/100/6 mm
5 connection flange, steel sheet metal, welded 15 mm
6 sprinkler line
7 steel profile L 80/80/6
8 steel pipe ⌀ 339/12,5 mm

Exhibition hall in Paris

Architects: Anne Lacaton & Jean Philippe Vassal, Paris

The multiple use hall, reminiscent of a giant greenhouse, offers an abundance of space for various events.

The new exhibition hall in the north of Paris is the first step in expanding the available exhibition area on site by 300,000 m². Since the large-scale structures are only used temporarily, the new trade show building was intended to provide for as many different uses as possible for other events and also be environmentally friendly and sustainable. The rectangular floor plan covers 189 × 78 m, and the hall is divided into two sections. A mobile partition wall can physically separate the two sections from each other and enables simultaneous, side-by-side operation. The northern part has a clear height of 12 m from floor to the underside of the roof construction,

and a column-free area of 72 by 78 m. For special events, a temporary auditorium with 800 to 2,000 seats can be installed. The southern area has a height of 9 m and a central row of columns. Utility and storage spaces are allocated as annexes measuring 3 m in height along the northern and western façade. The floors are laid out with concrete pavers that can support heavy loads. Underfloor ducts provide access to utilities and electronic media.

A double skin facade of corrugated polycarbonate panels envelopes the steel construction and permits natural illumination and ventilation. Vines can climb up along the steel frame between façade layers. The irrigation of planting, heat pump, and lighting are controlled centrally and are fully automatic.

Sections · floor plan
scale 1:1,500

1 Entrance
2 Exhibition area
3 Mobile partition wall
4 Utilities
5 Storage auditorium
6 Storage
7 Sprinkler depot
8 Reception exhibitors
9 Catering
10 Utility duct

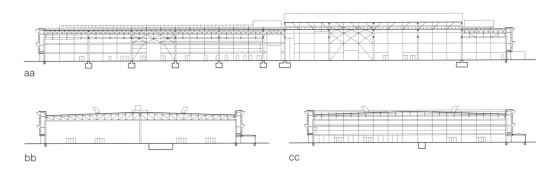

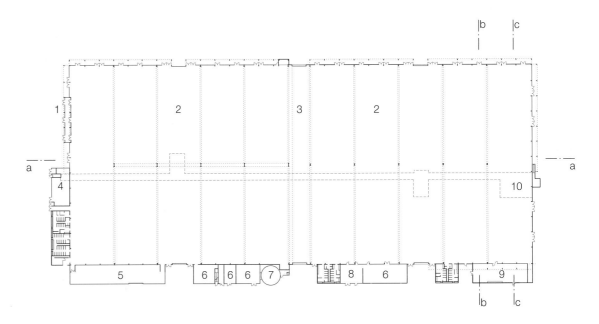

Project Data:

Use: trade show and exhibition hall
Construction: steel
Clear room height: 12 m (north)
9 m (south)
3 m (annexes)
Gross volume: 151,728 m³ (hall)
5,292 m³ (greenhouse)
8,132 m³ (utilities)
Gross footprint: 16,500 m²
Exhibition area: 15,000 m²
Total cost: € 15 million (net)
Completion: 2006
Construction time: 8 months

Schematics climate control
Summer/winter
scale 1:100

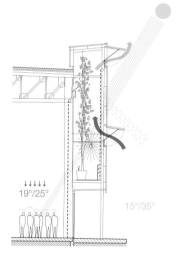

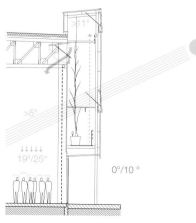

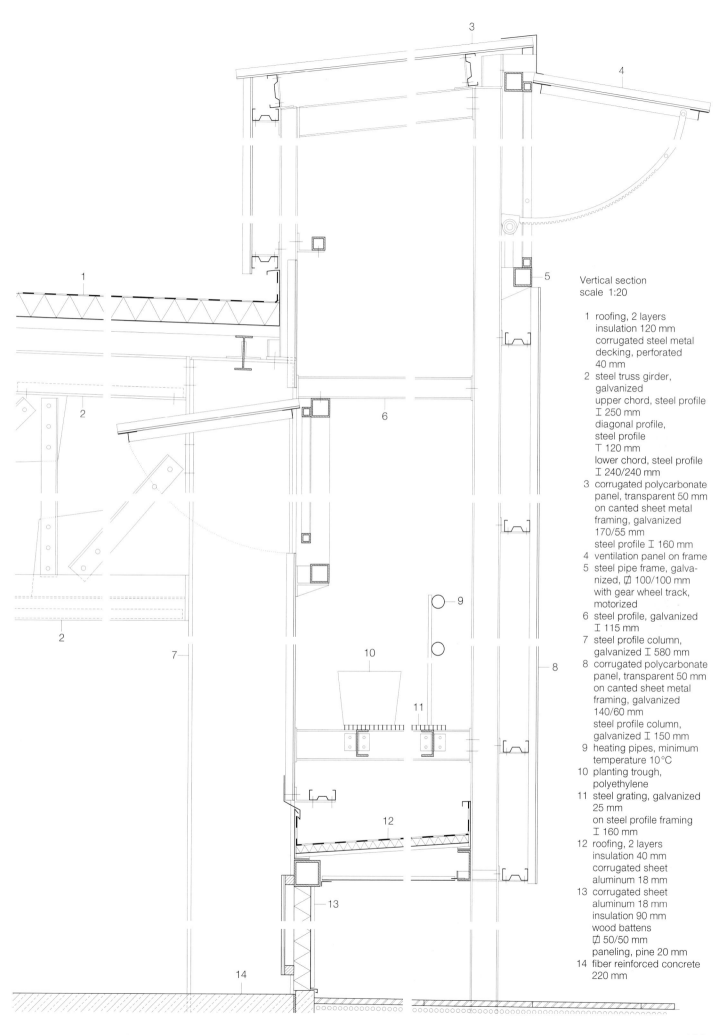

Vertical section
scale 1:20

1 roofing, 2 layers
   insulation 120 mm
   corrugated steel metal
   decking, perforated
   40 mm
2 steel truss girder,
   galvanized
   upper chord, steel profile
   I 250 mm
   diagonal profile,
   steel profile
   T 120 mm
   lower chord, steel profile
   I 240/240 mm
3 corrugated polycarbonate
   panel, transparent 50 mm
   on canted sheet metal
   framing, galvanized
   170/55 mm
   steel profile I 160 mm
4 ventilation panel on frame
5 steel pipe frame, galvanized, ⧄ 100/100 mm
   with gear wheel track,
   motorized
6 steel profile, galvanized
   I 115 mm
7 steel profile column,
   galvanized I 580 mm
8 corrugated polycarbonate
   panel, transparent 50 mm
   on canted sheet metal
   framing, galvanized
   140/60 mm
   steel profile column,
   galvanized I 150 mm
9 heating pipes, minimum
   temperature 10°C
10 planting trough,
   polyethylene
11 steel grating, galvanized
   25 mm
   on steel profile framing
   I 160 mm
12 roofing, 2 layers
   insulation 40 mm
   corrugated sheet
   aluminum 18 mm
13 corrugated sheet
   aluminum 18 mm
   insulation 90 mm
   wood battens
   ⧄ 50/50 mm
   paneling, pine 20 mm
14 fiber reinforced concrete
   220 mm

133

New Trade Fair in Stuttgart

Architects: Wulf & Partner, Stuttgart

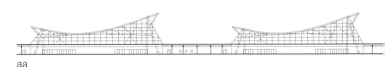

aa

The curved rooflines of the new trade fair, characterized by lightness and transparency, merge with the landscape in a harmonic way.

Designed by Stuttgart-based architects Wulf & Partner, a highly modern trade show environment was created featuring 100,000 m² total enclosed area, divided into eight trade show halls and one congress center. The spectacular parking garage with its green roof extends across the highway. The principles that the designers followed for creating this exceptionally large project comprised minimal land use, short walking distances, and an innovative visual appearance.

Topographic integration
The unmistakable character of the entire complex is created most of all by integration of topography within the trade show concept. Due to topographically related elevation changes, issues arose that benefited the project in terms of atmosphere and function. As result, every second hall can be entered at an elevated level. This not only provides for good orientation, but also spatial variety. The elevation changes not only result in the array of exhibition halls not being tiresome and monotonous in their visual appearance. The geometric offsetting also enables a better overview of the entire complex.

Green wave
The attractiveness of the new trade fair consists in the superimposition of clear shapes with vivid, free-form design. This is most of all apparent in the longitudinal section. Its motif is based on wave-like shapes, composed of the tensile roof

structures of the hall buildings and the slightly vaulted green roof of the parking garage building.
The central open spaces, "exhibition plaza" and "exhibition park", are important for the spatial organization of the complex. At the exhibition plaza, visitors can receive information on exhibition topics and events via integrated media facades.

Sensual material selection
The size and the high demands regarding visual appearance required discipline and coherence. The repetitive elements within the design vocabulary and material selection provide continuity. The material selection does not follow a superordinate principle, but is defined by location and function. In order to contrast the architecture with its engineering aesthetic, emphasis is laid on materials "that make sense", that are not only technically intelligent, but also appeal to touch, texture, and surface in a sensual way. The original color and character of materials are expressed throughout.

Architectural backdrop
Within the exhibition and event area, targeted illumination is provided laterally and from above. Large glazed surfaces create a dramatized relation between interior and exterior by exposing views towards the landscape. The delicate steel constructions provide an impression of lightness and graciousness. The architectural gesture offers a neutral backdrop for the lively trade show business and a background for other (exhibition-related) architectural interventions. Thus, minimal design, simplicity, and limiting material and structural elements are comprehensively employed design principles.

Project data:

Use:	trade show, exhibition, event halls and congress center
Construction:	steel
Clear height:	14 m (great hall)
	10 m (standard hall)
Gross volume:	3,000,000 m³
Gross footprint:	432,000 m²
Exhibition area:	100,000 m²
Total cost:	€ 806 million (gross)
Completion:	2007
Construction time:	38 months

Section   scale 1:2,000
Floor plan   scale 1:6,000

1 Great hall
2 Exhibition halls 1–7
3 Exhibition plaza
4 Congress center
5 Small exhibition hall
6 Large congress auditorium
7 Exhibition park
8 Entrance west
9 Entrance east
10 Parking garage

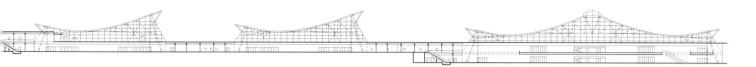

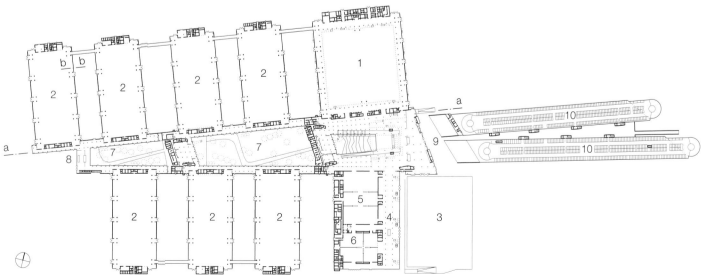

Vertical section standard hall
scale 1:50

1 stainless steel roofing, seam welded
  separating layer
  bituminous elastomer layer
  insulation, foamglass 10 mm with coating
  vapor barrier, bituminous, aluminum
  aggregate
  edge profile, steel box girder 900/180 mm
2 EPDM roofing sealant, root-proof
  insulation mineral fiber 140 mm
  vapor barrier, bituminous, aluminum
  aggregate 1.5 mm
  sheet metal, low gauge 1 mm

  steel metal decking 160 mm
3 tensile member, steel 150 mm
4 steel pipe ⌀ 660/30 mm
5 steel pipe ⌀ 457/20 mm
6 steel pipe ⌀ 508/25 mm
7 smoke and heat vent,
  bottom-hung window element,
  laminated glass
8 steel profile HEM 240
9 fixed glazing, laminated glass
10 opaque layer between facade posts
11 wall construction:
   aluminum coffer, framing
   ventilation 40 mm
   insulation, mineral fiber 20 mm + 140 mm

   steel sheet metal coffer 145 mm
   steel profile IPE 360
   Vierendeel truss, steel
   framing
   wood cladding
12 metal grating
13 cable channel, steel sheet metal,
   300/60 mm
14 floor construction:
   hard aggregate floor screed,
   power troweled 30 mm
   reinforced concrete floor/ceiling 470 mm
15 base flashing, canted edge, powder-coated
   ventilation gap 20 mm
   perimeter insulation EPS 60 mm

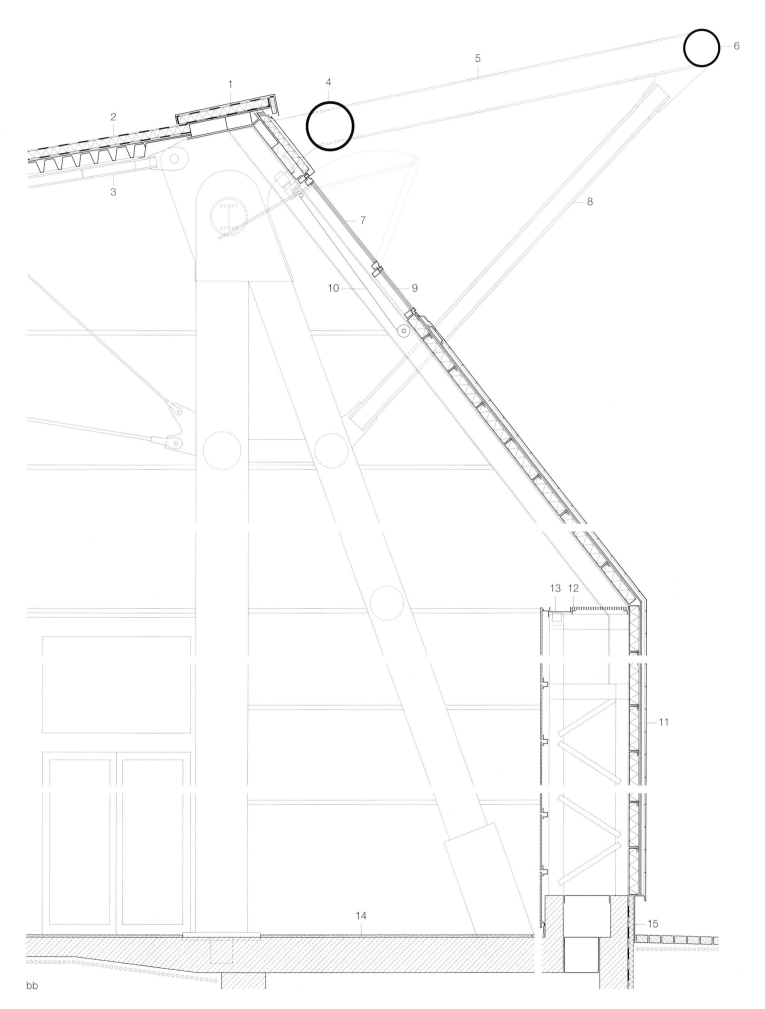

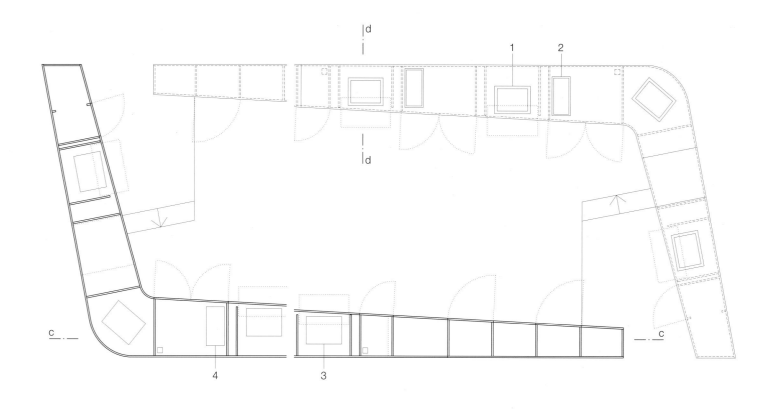

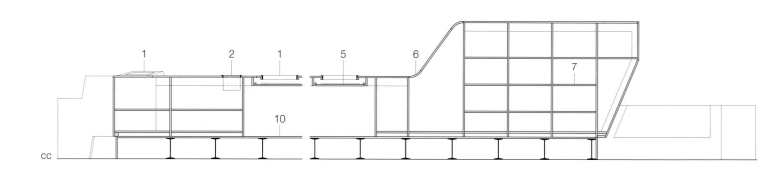

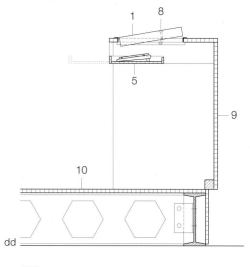

Information counter
Floor plan · section
scale 1:50
Vertical section   scale 1:20

1 recessed TFT-Monitor,
   framing: lateral aluminum └-profile 45/45 mm,
   facing flange 45 mm, monitor-to-frame bolt
   connection w/spacers
2 recessed scanner/ticket printer,
   flush to countertop
3 recess for monitor
4 recess for scanner/ticket printer
5 keyboard drawer: wood composite material,
   laminated, painted, steel ball bearing drawer
   tracks

6 composite wood material 20 mm
7 composite wood material, black laminate
   15 mm
8 steel lid hinge with spring joint and bend
   proofing
9 wood composite material, primed, painted,
   chamfered edges 20 mm
10 needle felt, adhered to
   wood composite 35 mm
   aluminum open-web steel beam
   I 280/120 mm as continuous frame with webs

Sustainably designing temporary architecture for brands

Susanne Schmidhuber

New space for brands

For some time now, an emergence of brand environments that are independent from flagship stores has taken place. A few years ago, fashion label Comme des Garçons marked the beginning of this development with their temporary guerilla-stores in deserted factory buildings. Two years later, the supermarket chain Wal Mart adopted this strategy, and brands such as adidas and Louis Vuitton followed. Today, so-called pop-up stores, temporary bars, and restaurants – mostly as cooperative lovechild of art and fashion – regularly attract well-networked metropolitans. In 2008 Comme des Garçons presented a whole new temporary concept: pocket-stores. Located in small retail spaces featuring a white box and placed between stores for every-day needs, they offer select fashion items of the label as well as its fragrance and accessory lines. The advantages of this new store concept are low rents, proximity to consumers' every-day life, as well as free advertisement via digitally distributed word-of-mouth information. This phenomenon however also indicates a fundamental development.

Types of business that don't usually deal with guerilla marketing and art are also on the lookout for new spaces. The automotive manufacturer Audi for instance participates in exhibitions such as Art Basel or the Design Annual in Frankfurt. For its exhibition stands, the Berker Corporation, producer of switches and electrical installation systems, cooperates with the renowned British artist Sam Taylor Wood.

All these advances by brands into the realm of temporary phenomena cannot only be understood as a reaction to the level of store rents or as a reflection of the popularity of art: They may also be understood as proof for the significance of brand spaces in new environments. This results in new opportunities and requirements for designers. Experiences and new spaces gain importance for corporations in the context of intensified global competition, rapid innovation, and the volatility of consumers. Crossover concepts and trade shows as well can benefit from this situation if they live up to the intrinsic demand for brand communication.

Changing trade shows

The continuous growth of the trade show industry since 2003 both in Germany and worldwide can also be interpreted as renaissance of its original significance. In 1240 AD Frankfurt received the first so-called imperial fair privilege from Emperor Friedrich II. The trade of goods and the competition among guilds and different cultures was originally held on a religious holiday (Latin: missa). This became very successful throughout Europe at that time and accelerated the development of brands: Trade associations and guilds determined that craftsmen should design their own symbols for registration in guild documents in order to trace back variations in quality to the manufacturer or sender. Trade shows became meeting places where people encountered brands. In 1895 the first sample trade show in Leipzig took place. Here, manufacturers delivered the ordered product quantity after the trade show. This procedure takes modern production means into account. In 1903 a stuffed bear with shaggy mohair fur and a button in his ear achieved an exemplary brand breakthrough: The presentation of the Steiff stuffed animal toy at the Messe Leipzig resulted in 12,000 orders. In the 20th century the trade show also became an important hub for technical innovations. In 1901 the Daimler-Motoren-Gesellschaft presented its new four-cylinder vehicle. In 1906 AEG introduced the first electrical cigarette lighter for cars at the trade show. Revolutionary innovations thus become tangible.

After 1950 the role of trade shows and brands changed, e.g. due to mediatization and its aftermath. Television became a powerful medium within the marketing mix. Telecommunication via the traditional media bloomed to the point of sensory overload. With traditional marketing channels losing importance, the orientation towards experimental or event marketing, generally defined as marketing via "sensual consumer experiences that are rooted in the emotional world of the consumer and influence their values, life styles, and attitudes"[1], began in the 1990s. Simultaneously, the Internet claimed the position of the leading medium in Europe.[2] This paradigm shift in media, communication, and consumption continues today. In addition to this, the significance of tangible experiences as such is changing, as the Internet has not only multiplied information but also disembodied it: Today, neither rustling paper nor the interaction with a conversation partner are present in the flow of information to people. The Internet as information medium limits traditional media, increases loss of interaction, and generates individualization of consumer habits. Per definition, communication in space counteracts this loss of a tangible component. However, brands need to do more at trade shows than simply roll out the red carpet, display their items, and put on the communicative hat. They need to initiate experiences. If trade shows used to be due diligence dates for exchange between merchants in the medieval era, then today corporations also need to exchange an immaterial value in combination with their products: a brand promise that extends far beyond the actual product. They need to provide visions for contemporary and future life style scenarios. The international automotive exhibition IAA for instance is literally at the forefront of mobility scenarios and receives its lifeblood today from the far-sighted character of "green" innovations and design.

According to the Association of German Trade Fair Industry (AUMA), trade shows have the opportunity to demonstrate their initial strength: visitors' personal experience of products and brands – especially considering the paradigm shift markets are currently subject to, and particularly in a weak economic cycle.[3] This aspect signifies the chances that trade shows and exhibition architecture possess in an accelerated and complex world. For one, it is a highly mobile instrument of guiding brands and of communication with dealers, as well as an indicator for the status quo and tendencies within a society. On the other hand, it promotes an individualized, autonomous mode of experience, characteristic for how contemporary Internet use increasingly influences consumer habits. However, these opportunities are met with a challenge: The business consultants Simonetta Carbonaro and Christian Votava warn that event marketing constitutes "senseless sensuality", placing emphasis on "brand experiences independent from intrinsic corporate identity."[4] This hints on the responsibility of design within the realm of temporary phenomena: Similar to built architecture, the focus is on the brand's identity, derived from the corporation's guiding principle, instead of volatile fireworks or signature pieces. It requires an emphatic creative vision for authenticity and change, since temporary architecture as medium of corporate architecture is meant to shape a brand's identity while establishing the potential for further development. Especially temporary architecture needs to consider brand design as sustainable process.

Towards a coherent design of experience
An exhibition presence has one chance for being successful. This opportunity arises when the visitor – drawn to the interior – enters: Visitors need to be able to immediately immerse themselves into the presentation, independently from how many innovations may require explanation. In the current school of brand management, brands are considered as having personalities or identities according to their soft image factors.[5] Sullivan's "form follows function" has been rephrased in regard to corporate architecture as "form follows identity". Within temporary architecture for brands, the dimension of being up-to-date comes into play as well. Brand environments within the roundabout of big exhibitions not only comprise built identity, but also need to display vivid gestures of this identity – phrased in some places as "form follows attitude."[6] Visitors need a central theme that helps them comprehend innovations and provides a coherent connection between a contemporary gesture and the content of the (mostly) familiar brand. Successful temporary brand spaces offer their audience – similar to good speakers – a recognition value, a basis for interpretation, a value system from which they venture forth into new realms after altering their audience's perception. The decisive factor for this is the seamless multidimensionality of the brand environment.

Multidimensionality and precision in a brand space
On the macro-level, multidimensionality begins inside the exhibition building with the impression an exhibition stand provides from a distance. By looking across the exhibition floor and through the aisles, a new realm has to make itself noticed – open enough to enter, closed enough to protect itself from distractions. When arriving at the exhibition stand, the visitors' transition to the inside needs to be seamless, into an attractive field of experience that separates them from the uproar and heterogeneity of the trade show. Especially for premium brands, this is a highly sensitive issue: Streams of visitors need to be subtly guided in order to make room for the interested clientele. Instead of hermetically closing off the brand, subtle spatial transitions are preferred. The first impression within the exhibition stand comprises the next step. It needs to immediately feel inviting to the visitors and emotionally prepare them for an in-depth brand experience. For this purpose, they need to be relaxed and move intuitively. The objective of the next layer is the communication of particular product highlights or services and thus guiding and maintaining attention. Vivid spaces alternating with strategic places for relaxation need to accommodate up to a million visitors in three exhibition days. People lining up before an exhibition stand may prove a brand's attractiveness. From the point of view of good exhibition architecture it is however considered a failure in planning that costs the brand potential visitors.

The holistic tasks of brand identity and the requirements of temporary use continue into a spatial micro level: good temporary design does not feel temporary. It combines the value of an ephemeral experience with the depth and seamlessness that characterizes good design. An intense brand experience can be hampered by tripping over flooring details and being distracted by LED grid design. Matteo Thun noticed in this regard that "the aesthetics of precision serve as qualification for the design of exhibition stands. They are not a value as such, not a formalistic demand devoid of content, but instead basis and at the same time result of each successful architecture of communication."[7] This precision is also the key to a brand's attitude, unfolding itself in the multidimensionality of space. Architecture needs to find a vanishing point in terms of content and meaning, enabling design in all its details to converge into a precise experience. This vanishing point is derived from the interdisciplinary abstraction of the relationship between communication and architecture.

A matrix for progressing brand spaces
Different than the similar disciplines of event communication and communication design, architecture for corporations and brands needs to translate marketing messages into a spatial, aesthetic, symbolic, and functional dimension. The briefing for an exhibition appearance is often situated between an abstract, communicative marketing message and very particular specifications for product presentation. Without translation however, these specifications result in a product parcours with a corporate identity look. The message that the space conveys, the content-based convergence point of design, is neither abstract nor concrete: It needs to lead together the briefing's abstract and the requirements at the level of meaning. This kind of convergence point is developed from viewing the claim for target groups in a greater perspective.

This is especially significant for rather abstract services that are difficult to advertise, such as in the case of the business consultancy group KPMG. For the CeBIT 2000 the claim "it's time for clarity", developed by the branding agency KMS Team, needed to be transformed into a spatial experience. Schmidhuber + Partner found the key to the design in a KPMG manager's statement: "You know, numbers live. These numbers tell us how healthy a company that we analyze is, its history, the possibilities of improvement, as well as its future." The communication aspect of "clarity" is translated into the architectural motif of translucency, permeated by the human factor: Binary codes on translucent exhibition partition walls are legible for visitors passing by. For this purpose, satinized glass panels are placed in 1 m distance to dark blue wall surfaces. Exhibition stand visitors passing through the aisles can thus penetrate the world of numbers and also become a living design element. The modulated transparency translates the brand message into space.

This seemingly easy pass is in reality the result of an intensive and interdisciplinary process that often includes in-depth research on the subject and relevant materials. Only in few cases this phase may last longer than eight weeks, as hardly more than six weeks are usually available beginning from the first briefing to the first trade show day on an international location. Concluding the creative process, a concept is established that equals a matrix in temporary architecture. Different from corporate architecture, the exhibition appearance of international brands needs to permit for changes and adaptations according to different exhibition locations. Sustainability is thus not a contradictory label of temporary architecture, but a requirement that pervades all levels of a concept.

On the level of physical design, the goal is to develop modules that can be used repeatedly. This, next to sophisticated logistics and storage of components, also demands innovative technical developments in construction, since modules can very quickly lose their design attractiveness if they in fact also inhibit it. Thus, the visibly recognizable connector mechanics of the Mero-system have temporarily led to uniformity in the basic structure of exhibition stands.

On the level of aesthetic design value, the goal is to reflect on a brand's design vocabulary both sensitively and in regard to tendencies in art, interior materials, and international design. Instead of pure zeitgeist of forms, a coherent interpretation of these tendencies within the context of the brand is preferred. A brand appearance always continues something that has taken place before. It needs to continue brand values in order to be further developed as such, whether opting for evolution or revolution of a brand.

Spatial revolution and evolution

In 1999 the Berker Corporation initiated a comprehensive relaunch of its corporate brand. It comprised changing the internal corporate structure, enhancing the core competencies, and developing a new corporate identity plus logo. In January 2000 the relaunch debuted. The main communica-

1   Audi exhibition stand, IAA Frankfurt, 2007
2   KPMG exibition stand, CeBIT Hannover, 2000

2

tion medium was the light & building trade show in March 2000 in Frankfurt. Schmidhuber + Partner were contracted to design the revolution of Berker's exhibition appearance. The task was to visualize Berker's existing competencies in the sectors of design and technology, according to the values of individuality, timelessness, humanity, and innovation. The objective was to set a signal of change, in harmony with the "down home" character of the corporation, located in Germany's Sauerland region. The inspiration for the new architectural matrix was developed equally via design and the innovative quality of the products, as well as the core of the enterprise: Following the principles of the Bauhaus, representing classic Modernism and as such architecturally reflecting Berker's brand values, Berker itself became a house. While past exhibition appearances used to be a series of changing designs grouped around switchboards and exhibition partition walls, the new stand comprises an open house.

The white residential cube is both central design element and construction module. Visitors can view the interior through horizontal facade apertures as if looking through a window. The strict reduction of exhibited products provides for placement of the switches just like in a real house. The interior design, minimal yet with a warm impression due to lighting and wooden floors, makes the idea of the Bauhaus something the visitors can respond to emotionally and already includes concepts for future variations of the dramaturgy: The seating offers views of white interior walls that provide a changeable scenery for content via media projection. In 2000 corporate consultant Thomas Biswanger, designer for Berker's new corporate identity and since then consultant for the company, marked the beginning of a courageous and sustainably relevant dramatization: He contracted the British photo and video artist Sam Taylor Wood, specialized in depicting people in every-day images of high density, for the innovative media projections of the interior walls. For the media walls of the exhibition stand, she designed widescreen projections that depict living in a loft as well as individual spatial existence.

Following its debut appearance in 2000 the Berker house is newly interpreted every two years. It grows and changes. Decisive for the continued validity of this exhibition appearance is its continued conforming to the corporate core values. Thus, the Berker house became a revolution in design that was capable of transforming into an evolution.

Brand space in progression
Designing the brand appearance for an automotive corporation in the premium market segment seems simple at first glance, considering it deals with highly innovative real-life products of great public interest. However, innovation and core competencies are situated closely together in the automotive business, a market that is fought over tougher than ever. All the more, designers need to materialize the brand into an independent, differentiated, and absolutely unmistakable experience for trade shows. From 1992 to the present, Schmidhuber + Partner in cooperation with Audi AG further developed Audi's spatial branding and also changed it: at international exhibitions since 2006 Audi displays an architectural vocabulary that began with an experiment.

Revolution from within

For Audi, the brand claim "Advancement through technology" is continually valid. It is based on the brand values athletic, progressive, and valuable. The revolution of the exhibition architecture strictly adheres to this and was initiated by a courageous excursion: In cooperation with Stylepark AG, Audi participated as the sole automotive manufacturer at the Design Annual, the annual event for high-end design of the Messe Frankfurt, in Frankfurt in 2006. According to the slogan "inside: urban", the newly developed Audi TT Coupé was exhibited.

5

For this purpose, the architecture adopted a notion from inside the corporation: The design vocabulary of the new TT developed by Audi – a combination of curved forms and sharp-edged angles – visualizes the brand's unmistakable orientation towards design. The concept for the trade show appearance explores its possibilities within the realm of the temporary to the fullest extent. For this purpose, it limited the brand value "athletic" for the first time, made use of "valuable" and emphasized "progressive". Thus, it defines the Audi TT as a modern nomad conceived for the urban environment, internationally at home within this context. The underlying thought is that its aesthetic progressiveness elevates it from the street parking lot and the garage; as a design object it receives a place inside the house that even perfectly envelopes the car.

6

For the most part, the exhibition stand is designed as an enclosed body demonstrating a compact appearance. Creating excavations within this body makes the new TT logo visible in accord with the vehicle's design vocabulary: curved shapes collide with sharp-edged angles. Within the interior, the color and tangible qualities are reversed. The limitation to only one surface material in white focuses the gesture of the space exclusively on the vehicle. Along the walls visitors view, as if looking through windows, at a city, an integrated media horizon, designed with projections from eleven international photo artists. The exhibition stand and the entire dramatization comprise a homage to an icon of design. For the first time, a defined, legible space has been developed for the vehicle presentation of Audi, in an experiment that dared implementing vehicular design components into an architectural brand message.

Evolution of terminal architecture

Two factors determine the further development of this exhibition concept for international exhibitions: For one, the basic idea of the TT-Loft was to create a definable, legible space for vehicle presentation. The concept was also intended to bridge the gap between the simultaneously developed dealership architecture of the Audi Terminals by Allmann Sattler Wappner Architekten – multi-story buildings designed for inner city locations (page 96–99). Originating in this conceptual idea, a striking urban structure was developed that includes the design vocabulary of round shapes and inclined, angular transitions: the Audi Exhibition Terminal.

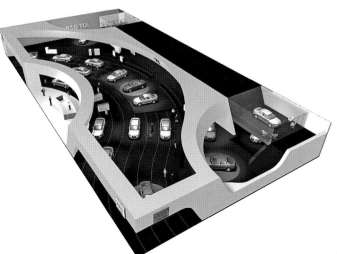

3–4 Berker exhibition stand, light + building Frankfurt, 2000
      projections by British artist Sam Taylor Wood (background)
5   Design study, headlights, Audi TT Coupé
6   Audi TT-Loft, Design Annual Frankfurt, 2006
7   Audi exhibition stand, Mondial de L'Automobile Paris, 2006

7

8

At the Mondial de L'Automobile 2006 in Paris Audi presented the world debut of the R8, the TT Roadster and the S3. Different than the Design Annual, the brand value "athletic" was given the spotlight once more, parallel to "progressive" and "valuable". In accord with the premium strategy, the exhibition stand became a flagship store in proximity to the street. The exhibition and the stream of visitors are defined by the architectural motif of the street, the curvature of which proceeds across the exhibition stand floor. The exhibition stand is circumscribed as a whole by the Terminal, providing a frame for the exhibition stand as well as its structure. It translates the idea of the street plan into a spatial form and constitutes the image of the exhibition stand from afar.

For the IAA 2007 in Frankfurt, the Audi Terminal architecture was subject to further decisive development. Planning and design of a brand space the size of the Audio exhibition stand at the IAA is comparable to a typical conceptual task in urban planning and design, given its floor area of 5,400 m^2 and a projected one million visitors. A further challenge at the Frankfurt exhibition location consisted in the fact that Audi does not occupy an entire space by itself and thus does not have a single brand environment such as e.g. BMW and Mercedes. The unmistakable definition as premium brand within the exhibition space thus becomes an architectural task.

In Frankfurt, the concept of the Paris terminal is concentrated into an urban market square, shielded from the bordering exhibition space and presentation surroundings. The delicate balance between openness and exclusiveness was developed in cooperation with Audi. The skywalk, a shining white floor and ceiling track that traverses the entire space, resembles a large sculpture (ill. 8). It is intended to draw visitors inside, to provide immediate orientation within the interior, and intuitively guide them through the displayed content. The high-tech stations placed along the skywalk and developed in cooperation with Mutabor Design introduce the technical innovations of the highlight, the A4, to the visitors and invite them to interact. By engaging visitors this way, they can delve into the next level of experience. Along the white trajectory of the skywalk, visitors reach the core of the exhibition stand: The showdrive, a glass screen that encompasses the space, reflects the image of the vehicle as if it was a jewel, and dramatizes it in a filmographic way. The steps of the highlight grandstand also serve as seating and invite visitors to watch and relax. From here, the exhibition stand can be experienced in its entirety (ill. 10).

The self-contained A4 Lounge is located at the end of the skywalk. Seating and ceiling follow the contours of the A4. Thus, the interior space of the lounge incorporates the dynamics of design and technology. The A4 seems to float through the black space as through a wind tunnel. The dynamic shapes of the seating, which mutates into the structure of the bar, were accomplished by special treatment of an acrylic based mineral compound material (ill. 9).

Sustainable design of multidimensionality and precision
The terminal serves as manifestation of dramatization and places high demands on structural design, construction technology, and craftsmanship. It requires column-free spaces as well as free-form construction components suitable for column widths of up to 20 m. Until now, the terminal

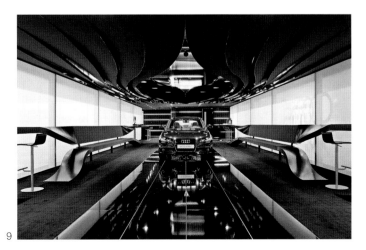

9

shell comprised traditional drywall construction with light-weight construction panels or membrane covering, according to what the most adequate surface material would be for a seamless visual appearance.

When balancing construction time and cost efficiency, a choice for location influences how much thought is put into finding solutions for quick and easy assembly before construction begins. For instance, at the North American International Auto Show in Detroit, assembly was very time-consuming due to strict trade union regulations. For the Peking Motor Show however, a detailed construction manual for assembly of components is important.

The objectives of Schmidhuber + Partner at the IAA in 2007 were to overcome the hitherto usual physical interfaces of media installation. An example for this is the LED-wall behind the highlight grandstand. In order to make the typical grid structure between LED modules invisible, yet not impair the image, parsol glass – a black tinted, but still transparent glass – was used. Individual graphics and video could thus be shown on the LED surface, moved across the absolutely homogeneous dark screen, and fade out into nothingness.

The choice of flooring material as well originates in the contextual matrix of this exhibition stand. The flooring material beneath the new A4, reminiscent of asphalt, was intended to emphasize the brand aspect "valuable" in order to take into account the Audi-typical exclusive features of newly purchased vehicles. In order to create the impression of glittering and visual depth, a new kind of layered flooring made of

silicium carbide was developed that, in its crystalline structure, reflects incoming light into all directions and thus added an additional atmospheric highlight quality.

Limiting the exhibition stand to high tech materials, the invisible integration of media, guidance of visitors, as well as the comprehensively tailor-made technology and materials were the constitutive elements of this exhibition appearance. Today the formal syntax of the Terminal's architecture, it's unmistakable form and color selection comprise a recognition value for the Audi AG at trade shows worldwide and permits the design of different adaptations for the different content-based core aspects of global exhibition appearances.

Temporary architecture as inspiration for 3D corporate design

Brands only become reality when consumers perceive and comprehend them. The telecommunications service brand Viag Interkom had already been awarded a prize for its exhibition appearance at CeBIT in Germany in 2001. After its cellular phone service was integrated into British Telecom's O_2 brand, the task was to introduce this brand, heretofore unknown in Germany, and provide it with a sensual basis. Its debut – even before the Germany-wide communications campaign started – took place at CeBIT 2002.

"Develop the home for a brand that does not yet exist." A thrilling task was presented to Schmidhuber + Partner and the brand agency KMS Team! Its origin was a corporate identity developed by the Lambi Naim Agency: the chemical formula for Oxygen, an indispensable, "elementary" component of our life, constitutes the logo for O_2, in white and deep blue colors, and formulates the brand values "open, bold, clear, trusted."

The O_2 brand's first space

The exhibition stand at the CeBIT 2002 was intended as an oasis of openness, transparency, and lightness within the hustle and bustle of the trade show. For this purpose, the entire presentation area was designed as a raised platform: Backlit from below, the O_2 exhibition stand "floats" 50 cm above the floor on top of a pedestal. While the exterior shell displays the two brand names, visible from afar, the interior is completely dedicated to communicating the new brand.

The interior of the 1,425 m² floor area of the exhibition stand is strategically divided into an active, vivid center area, an info bar for the individual discovery of products, as well as a calm border area consisting of individual lounges. Opposed to the usual principle of efficiency in guiding visitors, O_2 agreed to these bays for relaxing, serving as the brand's invitation to visitors to a personal consultation and into a relationship of trust, according to the market value "trustworthy". The length of stay at the exhibition stand and interviews with visitors conducted by the market research institute FairControl indicated that 85 % of exhibition stand visitors correctly remembered the message "Viag Interkom is called O_2 in the future", even though only half of them had prior knowledge of the rebranding. The 3D corporate design, elaborated for the

10

8–10 Audi exhibition stand, IAA Frankfurt, 2007

11

first time, had been integrated into the marketing of the corporation – and thus also into non-temporary spaces. From 2002 to 2005, a number of adaptations of the exhibition architecture were developed for the 3D corporate design of the O_2 corporation.

The O_2 Media Cloud

For the CeBIT 2005, the exhibition stand was intended to represent the continuously evolved significance of the O_2 corporation and brand. The emotion-based brand commitment and differentiation is thus placed into the foreground, prior to explanation and creating trust, matching the situation on the mobile phone market. In accord with this liberty, the floating horizon was further developed according to the subject of "open space", conceptually advanced as unlimited "outside", and interpreted as landscape with individual thematic islands.

The idea of the "sky" above the exhibition stand resulted from the demand for elevating what had previously been the "horizon" into the third dimension of space. This process resulted in the creation of a sculpture that was even four-dimensional: the O_2 Media Cloud. The sky above the O_2 landscape is not only intended to enclose and provide light, but also convey the innovation and the spirit of mobile communication – as intended by KMS Team. In close collaboration with KMS, Schmidhuber + Partner developed the idea of an LED screen with a surface of more than 1,000 m². To this day, no comparable project in exhibition architecture comes even close. 28,000 LEDs are placed 20 cm off center. Thus, the human eye perceives them as a single image from a distance. Each of the RGB LEDs of varying length are computer programmed. Their assembly is terminated by a diffuser made of satinized plastic. Thus, moving images are displayed on a screen that, like a blue cloud, floats above the heads of the exhibition stand visitors. As result, the media cloud not only comprises the world's largest color TV screen, but also an architectural sculpture that can display content and be interactively integrated.

The technology for the media cloud project, developed specifically for this project, was intended for use in Germany, the USA, and Taiwan, and until today adapted to three trade shows without any necessary construction modifications.

Following CeBIT 2005, this further development of the architectural concept for the O_2 exhibition appearance contributed to the company's 3D corporate design. The media cloud was newly interpreted by transforming the pixel landscape into large-scale light spots via an integrated lighting and LED wall. Today this media wall is used in the spaces of the company management of the O_2 "Uptown" administration building in Munich: Here, it characterizes the atmosphere of spaces at the heart of the corporation, showing images in blue light.

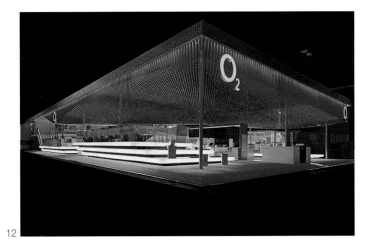

12

13

11   O_2 exhibition stand, CeBIT Hannover, 2002
12–13 O_2 exhibition stand, CeBIT Hannover, 2005
        thematic islands beneath media cloud "sky"
14   O_2 administrative building "Uptown", Munich, 2004;
        Ingenhoven Architects
15–16   "O_2 World on Tour", 2008

Cultural brand scenario: The "O_2 world on tour"

In autumn of 2008 the O_2 World Berlin opened its gates. The brand now hosts events in the most modern multifunctional arena in Europe, thus meeting its target audience within a cultural event scenario. Prior to the opening, O_2 utilized its core subject, mobility, in order to make this new host role known across Germany. A wandering temporary brand space hosted high profile live entertainment and guests in four German metropolises. For the "O_2 World on Tour" the goal was to translate the design quality of the exhibition appearances into a cost efficient, mobile brand space.

The design of the mobile pavilion houses the event space as well as infrastructural areas and operations offices, fused together by a 200 m long, free standing facade into a building volume that represents the brand. Through the entrance area, visitors reach the reception area and the event auditorium for up to 1,350 guests, as well as the VIP lounge with 140 m² floor area. Its individual, segmented integration into 25 containers serves as example for a design concept that took requirements of transportation, modification, and budget into account without employing the typical aesthetics of fragmented construction methods. The idea of "shrinking skin" served as conceptual goal for uniting the individual flexible components and functions of the wandering arena into a single structure. The exterior shell, a plastic membrane, can adapt to the pavilion by expanding or contracting. The construction itself is comprised of as many off-the-shelf, standard building components as possible, providing for an almost complete reusability of individual parts after service. With its modulated exterior shape and lighting design, the "O_2 World on Tour" evokes the image of a futuristic spaceship that has temporarily landed in the city.

14

Outlook

Temporary architecture in Germany is at an interesting crossroads in terms of economy and society. For German corporations, the international participation in trade exhibitions becomes more and more important in the context of globalization. The exhibition know-how developed here, and the culture of temporary phenomena, also comprise an international export item. Beyond that, temporary architecture can place corporations and brands into a new context: Within a mobile, event-oriented society, progressingly critical of marketing, it can create a bridge between space, communication, and culture.

15

1   Weinberg, Peter: Erlebnismarketing. Munich 1992
2   Cf. EIAA Mediascope Europe 2008 Studie: http://www.eiaa.net/
    research/media-consumption.asp. retrieved: November 2008
3   Cf. AUMA Presseinfo 17.11.2008: http://www.aumamessen.de/
    _pages/d/09_Presse/0901_PresseInfos/090102_Archiv/presse08/
    presse19-2008.html. retrieved: 18.11.2008
4   Carbonaro, Simonetta und Votava, Christian: Die Konsumenten haben
    eine tiefe Sehnsucht nach Authentizität. In: GDI Impuls, 03/2008, p. 85
5   Cf. Kilian, Karsten: Determinanten der Markenpersönlichkeit – Ansatz-
    punkte zur empirischen Erforschung von die Markenpersönlichkeit
    prägenden Einflussfaktoren. http://www.markenlexikon.com/d_texte/
    markendeterminanten_kilian_2004.pdf. retrieved: March 2004
6   Cf. Seelen, Ansgar: Form follows attitude. Brand Identity & Design
    der nächsten Generation(en). http://weblogs.mki.fh-duesseldorf.de/
    brandidentity/FormFollowsattitude_FHD_151208.pdf
7   Danner, Dietmar: Architektur als Marketingfaktor. 12 Wege zum
    Unternehmenserfolg. Leinfelden-Echterdingen 2002, p. 144

Collaboration: Melanie Schehl

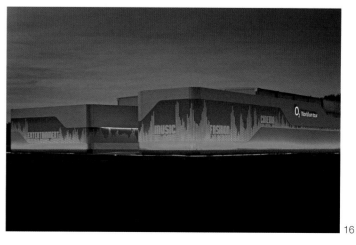

16

Stylepark Lounge in Berlin

Architects: J. MAYER H., Berlin

Project Data:

Use:	cultural/education
Construction:	engineered wood
Clear room height:	5 m
Exhibition area:	220 m²
Completion:	2001
Construction time:	3 months

Wave-like elements form a dynamic landscape and serve as seating, infotheque, and computer terminals.

At the XXI. World Congress of the Union Internationale des Architectes (UIA) and PlanCom 2002, the international trade show for planning professionals in the construction business, Stylepark AG presented its newest project, an interactive lounge. At the exhibited terminals, visitors were invited to try out a new tool for creative processes. The project creates new kinds of perception by emotional interaction and integrates visitors into a playful process. The temporary lounge was specifically designed for the UIA and PlanCom. However, its modular system also permits other constellations.

The lounge consists of a linoleum-covered and wave-like topography. The abstract forms serve as seating and workstations and thus meet different functional demands. Communication areas, lounge areas, video projections, and interactive elements merge into each other and connect all programmatic elements, creating a homogeneous, yet spatially structured constellation.

Thus, visitors are offered opportunities for both actively and passively gaining knowledge through computer terminals and projections. The conventional categories of furniture, wall, and multimedia thus are transformed into a communication landscape, both integrating its visitors and serving them. As result, immediate interaction between space and visitor is made possible.

aa

bb

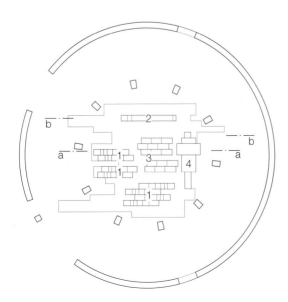

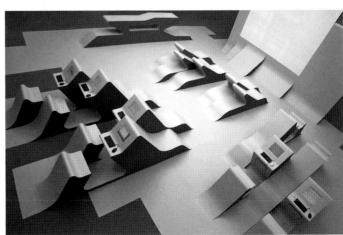

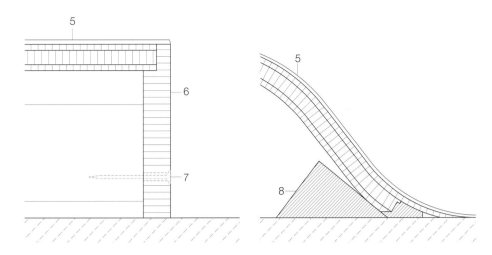

Sections · floor plan
scale 1:400

1 Internet
2 Infotheque
3 Lounge
4 Projection

Vertical sections   scale 1:2.5

5 linoleum 4 mm
   curved plywood 4 mm
   curved MDF 9.5 mm
   curved plywood 4 mm
6 MDF, primed and painted 19 mm
7 countersunk head, spackled, primed
8 wood blocking

Exhibition stand "Garment Garden" in Frankfurt am Main

Architects: J. MAYER H., Berlin

Tree-like fabric sculptures offer a place for relaxation within the hectic trade show environment.

For the first Design Annual in Frankfurt am Main, an exhibition appearance was developed for the textile manufacturer Nya Nordiska with the intention of exemplifying its design competence and power for innovation as well as presenting new perspectives in interior design with the products on display. The concept for the exhibition appearance adopted the subject of the trade show, "inside: urban – life, living, work".

Manifold shapes and relations

The goal was to offer a place for relaxation and inspiration for visitors within the hustle and bustle of the trade show, drawing inspiration for its visual appearance from the exhibited fabrics. The Garment Garden is comprised of three vertical columns with elliptical cross sections. Their shapes are reminiscent of miniature skyscrapers or tree structures. They are covered in pleaded fabric, which can be understood as "curtain wall" as well as tree bark. Each sculpture, up to 6.5 m tall, consists of five individual elements comprised of truncated cones differing in height and width as well as in design and texture of the selected fabric covering.

Mirrored shapes

The dynamics of the bizarre shapes are perpetuated in the curved, two color patterns of the flooring, but also the slanted cylinders of the seating, which in return correspond to the flooring colors. At the borders of the exhibition area, walls covered in mirror foil provide distortionless reflections of these shapes and thus create an endless "exhibition forest". Visitors are thus confronted with different simultaneous perspectives of each fabric sculpture. They move, according to the chosen perspective, within a park or an urban jungle.

Project Data:

Use:	exhibition stand
Construction:	steel
Gross footprint:	42 m²
Completion:	2006
Construction time:	2 months

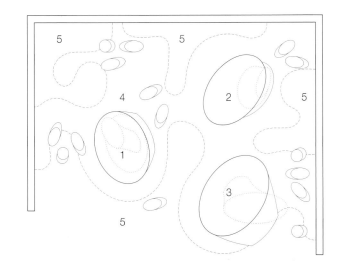

Floor plan   scale 1:100

1 Left tower
2 Central tower
3 Right tower
4 Flooring, fabric material
5 Textile flooring

Exhibition design system or custom design

Günther Röckl

Conventional building systems are the hot topic in our profession right now. Today, in the aftermath of the system boom of the 1970s and 1980s, only individual construction methods seem relevant. Of course, it's actually not that simple. Systems are certainly not rejected per se; even their most convinced opponents admit that exhibition design systems are justified to a particular, limited degree. Indeed, this is why the proponents of „custom exhibition architecture" don't deny the many advantages of good exhibition design systems – cost efficiency, reusability, flexibility, high quality design. Most of all, the cool appearance and lack of emotional quality is however considered the greatest weakness of these systems and is considered a contradiction to the necessity for giving an exhibition appearance an emotional character. But these discussions avoid the real subject and only serve those who want to see design exclusively as an art form. Yet actually nobody really wants to go that far – neither the exhibition builder nor in most cases the presenter, considering that exhibition appearances are expensive enough, even if only the most simple and cost efficient form of presentation is chosen.

Thus, the question arises: exhibition design system or custom design? One thing is certain. At exhibitions, it is important for an exhibiting corporation to use eye-catching exhibition architecture so the audience becomes interested in their exhibition appearance. Architectural solutions with appealing and individual design are thus an indispensable requirement in creating an exhibition appearance. And modern exhibition design systems are perfectly capable of meeting the demands set upon them.

However, whether in the past, the present, or the future, one fact remains the same: An exhibition design system is only as good as the designer who uses it. Or, in different words, designers will always choose the tools they need to tackle the task at hand, which fit into the scope of their envisioned concepts, which foster and support these, and are most of all affordable. The outcome finally proves whether there was a concept at all and if the comprehensive implementation of corporate identity in corporate design has been formulated and incorporated so market demands are met. In addition, one could argue that today's exhibition architecture should serve not only as symbol of the continuous succession of new products and services, but also the matching marketing concepts.

Past examples show us that exhibitors and designers first dealt with this problem when the tradeshow industry began its activity, and most of all in Germany – the country with the biggest exhibition design culture. Early on, following postwar rebuilding, people became aware that good products and services can only be presented within a particular framework. This can be seen as the birth of our contemporary exhibition design systems. Renowned designers such as Otl Aicher and Dieter Rams had dealt with this issue back then and created a sensation with their transparent and timeless exhibition architecture for the BRAUN corporation. And as the first exhibition design systems became available in the 1960s, they were considered revolutionary, since they symbolized all things modern and progressive in exhibition culture.

The comprehensive philosophy as basis of modern exhibition design systems, having developed from initial technological considerations via economic aspects to the momentary, design-oriented exhibition culture, originated in dealing with the transformative potential of space. Due to the fact that designs and the trends that are always one step ahead of them are subject to continuous change, modern exhibition design systems are forced to react to this transformative potential. In particular this means that an exhibition design system must adapt to these requirements in regard to available components, and needs to give the designer the ability to easily transform his ideas into tangible, spatial architecture.

Exhibition design systems were trendy back then, i. e. highly modern; yet today the exhibition design community is divided into two camps, as mentioned further above. However, in the discussions on „custom or system" in the last years, an alternative has emerged, last but not least due to the high costs of custom design. In the conflict between individuality and standardization, a third way emerges. Wherever cladding or paneling or finishing an exhibition design system is possible and makes sense economically, system technology finds use. Where the impression, i.e. show, is important, design-oriented and individual solutions are employed. Exhibition designers, architects, and designers have already made good experiences with such solutions. Therefore, this mixed design and construction method is on the advance.

The advantages of exhibition design systems
Without a doubt, modern exhibition design systems have many advantages, including for example flexibility, contemporaneousness and environmental impact.

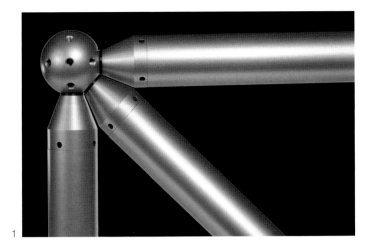

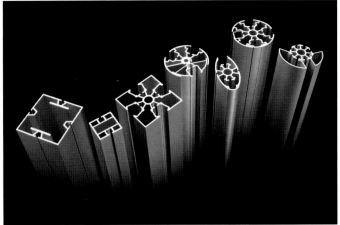

Flexibility

One of the most important preconditions and thus the main requirement for basic structures is to be variable to a certain degree. Lacking flexibility of use through e.g. components that can't be customized is not desired in exhibition design and for the most part too costly. However, if a seemingly geometrically fixed architectural framework provides for a play with correspondingly flexible construction elements, we call this a modular construction kit. If a system doesn't meet this requirement, it is simply not suitable as a system. However, the future objective will not be to simply offer the market standardized system components. System manufacturers today are already advancing in new directions and due to their high production capacity will be able to provide more individual components, i.e. more or less custom-made elements, by use of economical methods and at affordable prices.

Initial projects have already been implemented this way. The idea is to use the tried-and-trusted systems and their technology as basis in order to give them a new appearance over and over again, to provide them with state-of-the-art design, for instance by using modified connection technology, new materials, new finishes, etc.

Contemporaneousness

Contemporary architecture, i.e. in our case modern interior architecture, is an important standard for a concept and the related detail work. Current concepts in design and technology, most of all in the sector of architecture, require making a selection from a variety of diverse influences. The task of the designer is to channel these influences in order to provide the selected system with a contemporary appearance. This calls for system manufacturers as well to develop new and future-oriented systems based on these influences; systems that may be design-oriented and contemporary, yet still neutral enough as to not disturb the complexity of a product presentation by having an excessively vivid appearance.

Individuality

This criterion corresponds to people's increasing desire for assuming distinguished positions within society. This applies to our society as well as to exhibition architecture, its design, and the selected system. Architecture responds to this by creating an unmistakable and appealing character for exhibition architecture and thus also of events. A unique design in this sense requires flexibility of all those who contribute to

planning and construction – and finally, as result, from the selected system as well.

Valency

This term should play a significant role in the discussion between the client, i.e. the product, and the designer. The valency of exhibition architecture is intended to orient itself on the value system of the products on display, not more and not less. In general, architecture is not required to participate in establishing the character of a product, be it more or less valuable; however ideally supports it. The development of concepts for exhibition architecture is based on this recognition, as only the continuation of corporate identity guarantees the successful qualification and thus positioning of a corporation.

Environmental impact

The aspect of environmental impact is at least as important as the advantages described above. Longevity and reuse, i.e. recyclable raw materials provide the basis for every good exhibition design system. In this regard, high precision production technology with maximum energy efficiency is equally important as longevity of use.

Conventional construction methods	System-based construction methods
· no modular dimensions	· variable modules
· complex disassembly	· easy disassembly
· complex assembly	· quick assembly and disassembly
· low variability	· high variability
· mostly singular use only	· repeated use possible
· high shipping volume	· low shipping volume
· complex storage	· easy storage

3

1 Modular post/connection-construction system
2 Different profile sections, aluminum profile system for exhibition stand and retail interior construction
3 A short comparison of two construction methods

Eternit exhibition stands in Stuttgart and Munich

Architects: Astrid Bornheim Architektur, Berlin

The exhibition stands intended as communication platforms simultaneously present the products of the exhibiting company as both building materials and exhibits.

The exhibition stands designed by Astrid Bornheim for a leading European manufacturer of building materials were presented at the Dach & Holz 2008 trade show in Stuttgart and the Bau 2009 in Munich. They are completely made of fiber-cement panels and are intended as communication platforms with an inviting character. They serve for presenting product innovations. Also, the different uses of fiber-cement for roof, facade, interiors, and design can be demonstrated.

"Dach & Holz", Stuttgart

The 480 m² area of the exhibition stand at the trade show in Stuttgart features a red exterior, signaling the company's presence. In the interior however, cream white tinted fiber-cement panels are used, creating an impression of particular graciousness. The stylized red roof elements of the stand seem detached from the exhibition architecture; they float above the seemingly generous space, accentuate it and serve as sign post.

The exhibition architecture is closed off towards the exterior, however provides access and views into the stand's interior in selected places. Illuminated white display cases provide effective lighting for product models. 16 ceiling, wall, and floor system models are on the center stage, offering a view of construction methods and material composition. Consultation counters where visitors can receive information

on the company's product portfolio are integrated into the exhibition. A generous lounge with 50 seats and a 10 m long bar in the center of the stand complement the communication concept. The goal here was not to create a conventional, typical exhibition stand, but trade show architecture with particular sophistication.

"BAU", Munich

The exhibition stand at the BAU 2009 in Munich as well is simultaneously showroom and lounge and invites visitors to discover Eternit's diversity of materials.

A black "wall of fame" presents new products for ceiling, facade, and interior construction. It envelops the shining white "hall of fame", designed as a lounge area. There is no product exhibition within this communication area. Instead, a bar offers a place for personal consultations. The bar as well as the lounge benches are completely made of fiber-cement. Thanks to a towering, 4 m tall bowl made of white tinted fiber-cement panels, the exhibition stand is easily recognizable from afar. The exterior of the exhibition stand, comprised of charcoal tinted walls, is intended as a "petting wall" of sorts, offering surprising tangible experiences. It invites visitors to touch and explore and enables them to experience the different materials and surfaces. Also, it provides intriguing views towards inside and outside of the exhibition stand through generous apertures. The exterior shell leads visitors into the interior of the 300 m² area of the exhibition stand, in which new products of the company are presented within open showcases integrated in the charcoal tinted wall, displaying both origin and future of this building material.

Project data (Stuttgart exhibition stand):

Use:	exhibition stand
Construction:	fiber-cement board, wood
Clear height:	4.30 m
Overall height:	7.50 m
Gross footprint:	450 m²
Completion:	2008
Construction time:	5 days

Floor plan (Stuttgart)
scale 1:250
Diagram, assembly

1 Conference rooms
2 Lounge
3 Bar
4 Kitchen
5 Consultation counter
6 Model for floor assembly
7 Backlit counter
8 Models with roof components
9 Back office
10 Models with wall components

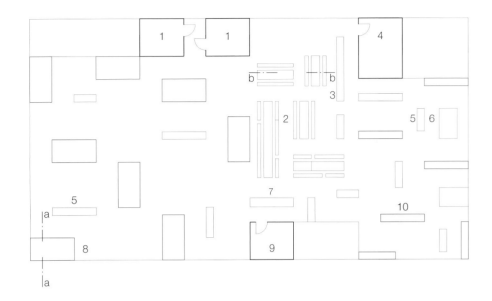

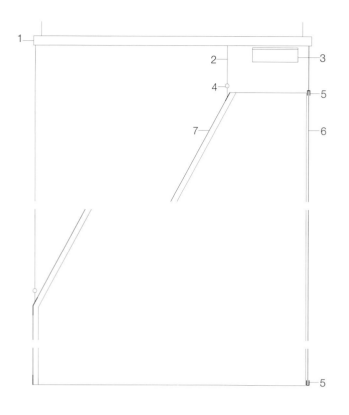

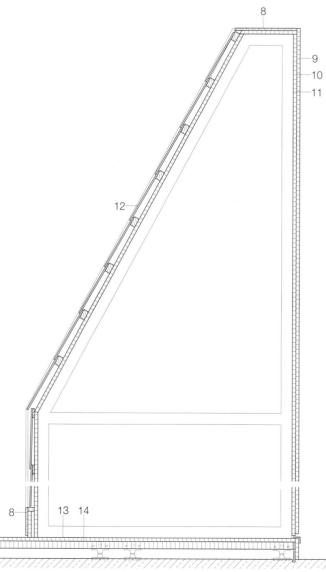

Vertical sections
roof exhibition and lounge area (Stuttgart)
scale 1:20

1 steel pipe
2 suspension, steel cable
3 RGB light fixture
4 steel grommet welded to steel angle,
  bolted to display case framing
5 Keder track, aluminum
6 fabric, red print, partial graphic print
7 square profile, aluminum, partially reinforced
  by wood panels, white fabric cover
8 facade panel, fiber-cement cream white 12 mm,
  laminated MDF substrate 19 mm
9 wood panel, red laminate
  (only exterior border models) 19 mm
10 MDF 19 mm
11 wood framing
12 exhibit (here: roofing and facade panels)
13 wood panels, white or grey laminate 19 mm
14 raised flooring system, for leveling and
  installations, system panel 38 mm
15 fluorescent lighting strip
16 framing, MDF, white fabric cover
17 MDF, red laminate 19 mm
18 cushion, white artificial leather upholstery
19 facade panel, fiber-cement cream white 12 mm

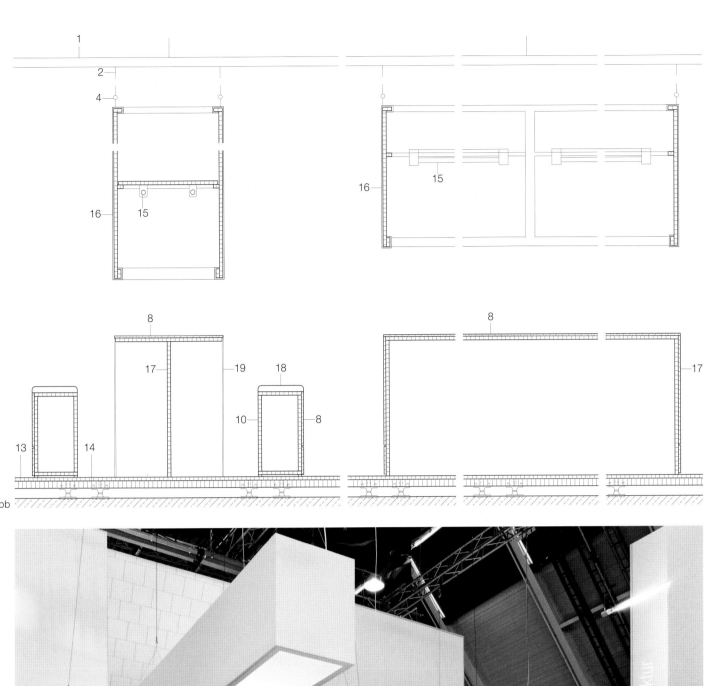

bb

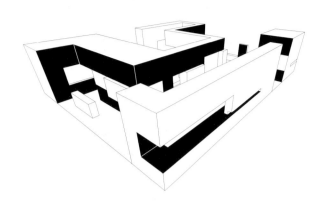

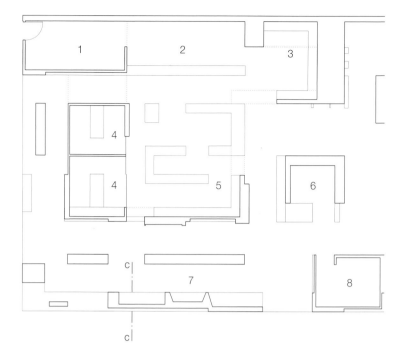

Project Data (Munich):

Use:	exhibition stand
Construction:	fiber-cement panels, wood
Clear room height:	2.50 m
Overall height:	3.75 m
Footprint:	310 m²
Completion:	2009
Construction time:	8 days

Perspective drawing (Munich)
Floor plan   scale 1:200

1 Kitchen
2 Bar
3 Small lounge
4 Conference
5 Lounge
6 Reception
7 Exhibition
8 Back office

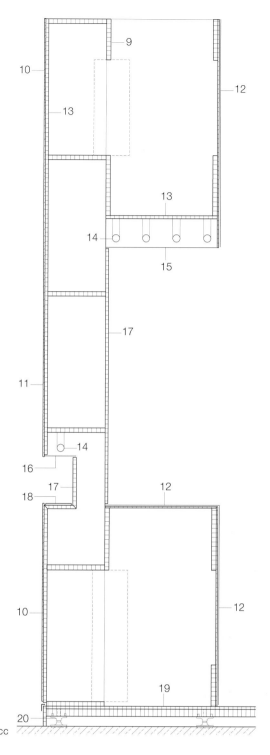

Vertical section (Munich)
scale 1:20

9 framing, plywood 24 mm
10 facade panel, fiber-cement creme white 8 mm,
on MDF substrate, laminated
11 facade panel, fiber-cement creme white 8 mm,
laminated on MDF substrate, millwork 3 mm depth
12 MDF 8 mm, fabric cover, black paint finish
13 MDF 16 mm
14 fluorescent lighting strip
15 acrylic glass, translucent white 10 mm
16 acrylic glass, translucent white 3 mm
17 MDF, black paint finish 16 mm
18 exhibit (here: demonstration sample,
facade panel)
19 wood panels, laminated white or black
20 raised flooring system for leveling and
installations

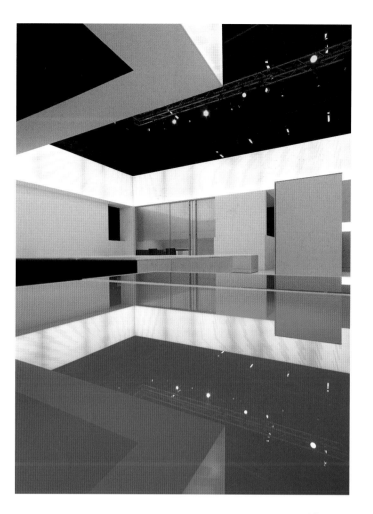

E.ON exhibition stand in Essen

Architects: avcommunication, Ludwigsburg/Munich

Dynamic design and clear separation between zones characterize the joint appearance of different corporate divisions.

The first joint exhibition appearance of the three corporate divisions E.ON Energy Sales, E.ON Ruhrgas, and E.ON IS at the E-world energy & water, Essen, called for an architectural concept that would represent the corporation as well as the three individual exhibitors.

Visitors are impressed by the exhibition stand's clear, open, and inviting visual appearance. Placed on the surface of the exhibition stand's white exterior, the shining red logo is visible from afar. Changing elevations and intersections of lines symbolize momentum and interrelations of the three divisions and emphasize the slogan "E.ON – solutions for a dynamic world."

Corporate presentation

The 1,075 m² area of the exhibition stand is clearly organized into different areas. In the exterior area, an arcade that circumscribes an open conversation zone serves to introduce the corporation. This part of the stand functions as meeting point and information forum, and this is where the different corporate departments present themselves individually at separate counters. The bar located in the middle of the exhibition stand is freely accessible and has an inviting character. Presentation counters, bars, and seating alcoves are backlit from below. This creates a light and floating visual impression. Walls and ceilings of the exhibition stand as well as the furniture consist of painted and laminated panels. The presentation counters are partially equipped with mirror-covered bases.

Communication areas

The reception desk is the central point of contact for customers and serves also as "access portal" to the more exclusive interior area. This zone is separated from the exterior area by backlit fabric walls. The secluded interior offers invited guests a protected environment for confidential conversations and conveys an exclusive lounge character. An atmosphere of concentration is created by the restrained design with its white surfaces and furniture. The dynamically curved ceilings in the lounge area contrast the otherwise strict design. Four laterally annexed conference rooms serve as presentation rooms for larger customer groups and offer opportunity for conversation within a spatially separate setting, far away from the trade show noise.

Project Data:

Use:	exhibition stand
Construction:	particle board
Clear room height:	5 m
Gross volume:	4,500 m³
Gross footprint:	1,075 m²
Exhibition area:	900 m²
Completion:	2008
Construction time	20 days (pre-assembly)
	7 days (assembly)

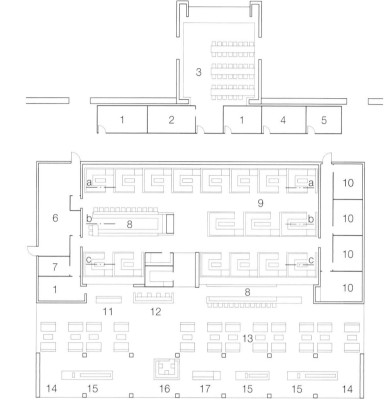

Floor plan   scale 1:400

1 Storage
2 Employee wardrobe
3 Employee room
4 Exhibition stand management
5 Board of Directors
6 Kitchen
7 Utilities
8 Bar
9 Interior lounge area
10 Conference
11 Recruiting
12 Reception
13 Exterior lounge area
14 Brand wall
15 Presentation counters
16 Information
17 Promotion and giveaways

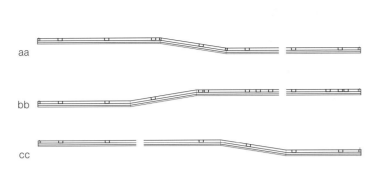

aa

bb

cc

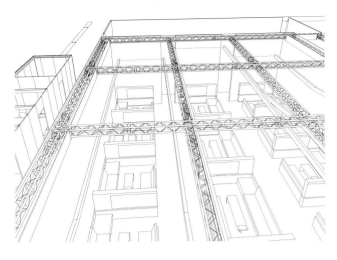

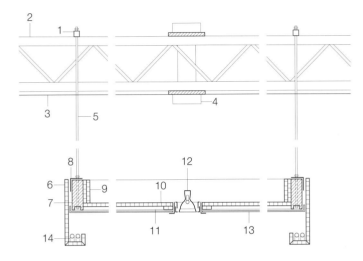

Vertical sections ceiling   scale 1:250
Perspective drawing, interior lounge area
Vertical section ceiling   scale 1:20

1 steel pipe ⌀ 30/30 mm
2 4-point aluminum truss system
3 molton, black
4 ventilator, visible parts black
5 threaded bar M8, painted black
6 particle board 19 mm
7 laminated timber construction 60/160 mm
8 aluminum angle 50/50/3 mm, pre-assembled to facing
9 veneer plywood, laminated 2× 19 mm
10 particle board, U-assembly, laminated 290/141/19 mm
11 ventilation gap 19 mm
12 halide metal vapor lamp
13 molton, white 330 g
      shirting fabric, white 220 g
14 fluorescent strip lighting, pre-assembly

Serafini exhibition stand in Cologne

Architects: atelier 522, Markdorf

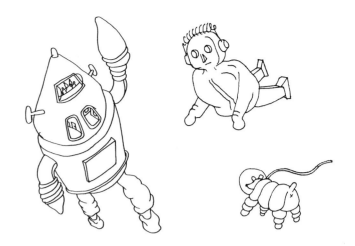

For the international furnishing show IMM, the design firm Serafini selected cool wall graffiti as guidance system for presenting their products.

Serafini represents contemporary product design for interior and exterior and manufactures, among others, individual shop, shelving, partition, and presentation systems. The company's new exhibition stand for the international furnishing show IMM 2009 in Cologne resembles a piece of art. The client's desire to achieve a significant effect with simple means presented a special challenge for the designers. With as few means as possible, the exhibition stand rejects futuristic design as well as laboriously designed lounge and conference areas, with the presentation of products being all that remains. The 112 m² area of the space, open on two sides, consists of no more than a floor slab and two 4.5 m tall wall partitions.

Dramatization of products in speech bubbles

The architects decided against recreating a residential scenery and concentrated on dramatizing the individual products. These are placed on speech bubbles adhered to simple, unfinished particle boards, and dramatized by young, futuristic illustrations in the style of comics. An artist painted the figures on site, projected by beamers onto the walls.
The exhibition elements are deliberately placed along walls at different heights. From a distance, visitors are thus impressed by the exhibition stand's visual appearance, yet are also invited to look at the displayed products up close, to touch them and try them. Thus, Serafini western stools became "discussion islands" on which client consultations could take place, in a relaxed atmosphere – calm, yet at the same time within the hustle and bustle of the trade show.

Project data:

Use:	exhibition stand
Construction:	particle board
Clear height:	4.5 m
Exhibition area:	110 m²
Completion:	2009
Construction time:	4 days

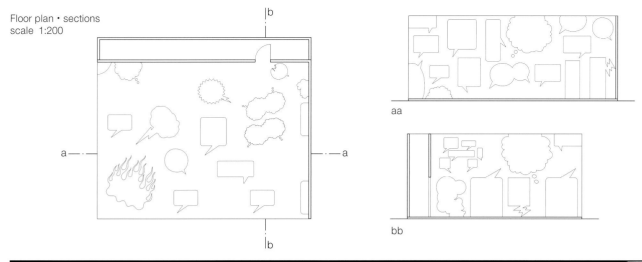

aa

bb

Architects – Project data

Phaeno Science Center in Wolfsburg

Client: City of Wolfsburg
Architects: Zaha Hadid Architects, London and Mayer Bährle Freie Architekten BDA, Lörrach
Project architect: Christos Passas
Assistant project architect: Sara Klomps
Exhibition design: Ansel Associates Inc., Point Richmond
Structural engineer: Adams Kara Taylor, London in collaboration with Ingenieurgruppe Tokarz Frerichs Leipold, Laatzen
Mechanical engineer: NEK Ingenieurteam, Wolfsburg GmbH, Wolfsburg
General planner and project management: Neuland Wohnungs-gesellschaft, Wolfsburg
Lighting planning: Fahlke & Dettmer, Neustadt in collaboration with Office for Visual-Interaction, New York
Completion: 2005

www.zaha-hadid.com
mail@zaha-hadid.com
www.mayer-baehrle.com
info@mayer-baehrle.com

Zaha Hadid
Born 1950, Baghdad; 1972–77 studies, Architectural Association, London; collaboration, Office for Metropolitan Architecture, Rotterdam; 1980–present Zaha Hadid Architects, London; until 1987 teaching position, AA in collaboration with Rem Koolhaas and Elia Zenghelis; 1987–present various teaching positions, currently Professor, University of Applied Arts Vienna.

New Museum in New York

Client: New Museum of Contem-porary Art, New York
Architects: SANAA/Kazuyo Sejima + Ryue Nishizawa, Tokyo
Project team: Florian Idenburg, Toshihiro Oki, Jonas Elding, Koji Yoshida, Hiroaki Katagiri, Javier Haddad, Erika Hidaka; Fenna Haakma-Wagenaar, Tetsuo Kondo, Taeko Nakatsubo
Partner architect: Gensler, New York; Madeline Burke-Vigeland, William Rice, Karen Pedrazzi, Kristian Gregerson, John Chow, Will Rohde, Sohee Moon, Christopher Duisberg, Edgar Papazian
Construction management: Sciame, New York
Structural engineer: Guy Nordenson and Associates, New York; SAPS – Sasaki and Partners, Tokyo
Mechanical engineer: Arup, New York
Facade design: Simpson Guperts & Heger, New York
Lighting planning: Tillotson Design, New York
Completion: 2007

www.sanaa.co.jp
sanaa@sanaa.co.jp

Kazuyo Sejima
Born 1956, Ibaraki Prefecture, Japan; 1981 Masters Degree, Japan Women's University Tokyo; 1987 founding of architecture office Kazuyo Sejima & Associates, Tokyo; 2001–present Professor, Keio University

Ryue Nishizawa
Born 1966, Kanagawa Prefecture, Japan; 1990 Masters Degree, Yokohama National University; 2001 Assistant Professor, Yoko-hama National University 1995 founding of SANAA

Literature Museum in Marbach

Client: Deutsches Literaturarchiv Marbach
Architects: David Chipperfield Architects, London/Berlin
Project manager: Alexander Schwarz
Project team: Harald Müller, Martina Betzold, Barbara Koller, Laura Fogarasi, Hannah Jonas
Construction management: Wenzel + Wenzel, Karlsruhe
Structural engineer: IGB – Ingenieurgruppe Bauen, Berlin
Exhibition design: Gestaltungsbüro element, Basle
Media planning: iart ineractive ag, Basle
Lighting planning: Mati AG, Adliswil, Switzerland
Completion: 2006

www.davidchipperfield.co.uk
info@davidchipperfield.co.uk

David Chipperfield
Born 1953 in London; 1977 Diploma, Architectural Association London; collaborator for Douglas Stephen, Richard Rogers, Norman Foster; 1984 founding of David Chipperfield Architects

Museum of Celtic and Roman History in Manching

Client: Zweckverband Keltisch-Römisches Archäologiemuseum Manching
Architects: Fischer Architekten, Munich
Project managers: Markus Klein, Sibylle Egger
Project team: Jan-Frederik Peters, Markus Seifert, Stefan Knoblauch, Hubert Wagner
Construction management: Thomas Rückert, Munich
Structural engineer: Mayr + Ludescher, Munich
Landscape architect: Anna Zeitz, Munich
Lighting planning: Michael Schmidt, Munich
Completion: 2006

www.fischer-architekten.com
info@fischer-architekten.com

Florian Fischer
Born 1965 in Munich; 1986–1994 architecture studies, TU Braunschweig, Southern California Institute of Architecture Santa Monica; Diploma, University of Stuttgart, Masters Degree, Columbia University New York; collaboration for UNStudio, Amsterdam; 1996–2002 partnership with Erhard Fischer, Munich, 2002–present Fischer Architekten, Munich

Alexandra Zeilhofer
Born in Munich; 1987–1992 architecture studies, Munich University of Applied Science; collaboration for Anderson Manson Dale Architects, Denver and Wilfried Mayer, Munich; 2002–present Fischer Architekten, Munich; 1998–present scenographic assistant for film and TV productions

BMW Museum in Munich

Client: BMW AG, Munich
General planner museum: ATELIER BRÜCKNER GmbH, Stuttgart
Creative Director: Uwe R. Brückner
Project manager: Eberhard Schlag
Facade and mechanical systems renovation: ASP Schweger Assoziierte Gesamtplanung GmbH, Hamburg
Structural engineer: Schlaich Bergermann und Partner, Stuttgart
Media scenography and interactive installations: ART+COM AG, Berlin
Visual symphony: TAMSCHICK MEDIA+SPACE GmbH
Graphic design, visual identity: Integral Ruedi Baur, Zurich
Lighting planning: Delux AG, Zurich
Completion: 2008

www.atelier-brueckner.com
kontakt@atelier-brueckner.com

Uwe R. Brückner
Born 1957; 1978–1984 architecture studies, TU Munich; studies in costume and set design, Stuttgart State Academy of Art and Design; collaboration for Sampo Widmann, Munich and Atelier Lohrer, Stuttgart; 1997 founding of ATELIER BRÜCKNER, Stuttgart; 2003–present Professor for Exhibition Design and Scenography, Basle School of Design

Eberhard Schlag
see p. 175

Mercedes-Benz Museum in Stuttgart

Client: DaimlerChrysler AG, Stuttgart
Architects: UNStudio, Amsterdam
Ben van Berkel, Tobias Wallisser, Caroline Bos
Project and construction management: UNStudio, Amsterdam, Wenzel + Wenzel, Stuttgart
General planner, museum content and design: hg merz architekten museumsgestalter, Stuttgart/Berlin
Structural engineer: Werner Sobek Ingenieure, Stuttgart; Boll und Partner Ingenieurgesellschaft mbH & Co. KG, Stuttgart
Lighting planning: Ulrike Brandi Licht, Lichtplanung und Leuchtenentwicklung GmbH, Hamburg
Electrical engineer: Werner Schwarz GmbH, Stuttgart
Mechanical engineer: Transplan Technik-Bauplanung GmbH, Stuttgart
Completion: 2006

www.unstudio.com
info@unstudio.com

Ben van Berkel
Born 1957 in Utrecht; 1987 Diploma, Rietveld Academy, Amsterdam and Architectural Association, London; Professor, Städelschule Stuttgart

Caroline Bos
Born 1959 in Rotterdam; 1991 B.A., Birkbeck College, London; guest lecturer i.a. Arnhem Academy of Architecture, Academy of Fine Arts Vienna

1988 founding of Van Berkel & Bos Architectuurbureau, Amsterdam; 1998–present UNStudio (partners: Tobias Wallisser, Harm Wassink)

"The Rommel Myth" exhibition in Stuttgart

Client: Haus der Geschichte Baden-Württemberg, Stuttgart
Architects: Hans Dieter Schaal, Attenweiler
Project team: Armin Teufel, Melanie Brugger
Graphic design: Lahaye Design, Ulm
Exibition construction: Heinzelmann GmbH & Co. KG, Mühlacker
Graphics reproduction: Oschatz Visuelle Medien, Wiesbaden
Media production: jangled nerves GmbH, Stuttgart
Completion: 2009

www.hansdieter-schaal.de

Hans Dieter Schaal
Born 1943 in Ulm/Donau; 1965–70 architecture studies, Hannover and Stuttgart; 1983 founding of Atelier and Office Hans Dieter Schaal, Attenweiler; active as architect, exhibition designer, set designer, landscape architect, artist, and author in Attenweiler/Ulm and Berlin

"That's Opera" traveling exhibition

Client: Ricordi & C. SpA, Milan
Promoter: Bertelsmann AG, Gütersloh
Architects: ATELIER BRÜCKNER GmbH, Stuttgart
Creative Director: Uwe R. Brückner
Project manager: Birgit Kadatz
Content research and exhibit logistics: Institut für Kulturaustausch, Tübingen
Media design, hardware: medienprojekt p2 GmbH, Stuttgart
Lighting design: LDE Belzner Holmes, Heidelberg
Media design: jangled nerves GmbH, Stuttgart
Completion: 2008

www.atelier-brueckner.com
kontakt@atelier-brueckner.com

Uwe R. Brückner
see p. 169

Birgit Kadatz
Studies in art history, Diploma as music theater director, University of Music and Theatre Hamburg; 1999–2005 Stuttgart National Theatre; 2000–2008 lecturer for dramaturgy and scenic education, Stuttgart State Academy of Art and Design; 2005–present collaborator for ATELIER BRÜCKNER

"Inventioneering Architecture" traveling exhibition

Client: ETH Zurich
Architects: Instant Architecture, Zurich; Dirk Hebel, Jörg Stollmann
Project team: Sascha Delz, bias Klauser, Martin Lüthy
Contractor: Bach Heiden AG, Heiden
Digital implementation: design-toproduction GmbH, Zurich; Markus Braach, Fabian Scheurer, Christoph Schindler
Completion: 2005

www.instant-arch.net

Dirk Hebel
Born 1971 in Birkenfeld/Nahe; 1998 Master of Architecture, ETH Zurich; 2000 Master of Architecture, Princeton University; collaboration for Diller+Scofidio, New York; 2002–present lecturer at ETH Zurich; 2007–2008 guest professor, Syracuse University, New York

Jörg Stollmann
Born 1969 in Düsseldorf; Architecture studies, TU Braunschweig, Berlin University of the Arts, Princeton University; collaboration for Atelier Seraji, Paris and Axel Schultes, Berlin; 2002–2008 scientific collaborator and teaching position, ETH Zurich; 2008–present guest professor, TU Berlin

2002-2008 joint architecture office, Instant Architecture

Museum pavilion in Pouilly-en-Auxois

Client: Institut du Canal & Halle du Toueur, Pouilly-en-Auxois
Architects: Shigeru Ban Architects, Tokyo/Paris
Project team: Anne Schéou, Damien Gaudin
Project management: Jean de Gastines, Paris
Structural engineer: Terrell Rooke et Associés, Paris; Peter Terrell, Eric Dixon
Mechanical engineer: Noble Ingénierie, Angers
Completion: 2004

www.shigerubanarchitects.com
tokyo@shigerubanarchitects.com
europe@shigerubanarchitects.com

Shigeru Ban
Born 1957 in Tokyo; 1978–1980 studies, Southern California Institute of Architecture (SCI-Arc) Santa Monica, USA; 1980–1982 Cooper Union School of Architecture New York; 1985 founding of Shigeru Ban Architects, Tokyo; 2000 guest professor, Columbia University New York; 2001–2008 Professor, Keio University Tokyo

Exhibition pavilion for Artek in Milan

Client: Artek, UPM, Milan, Italy
Architects: Shigeru Ban Architects, Tokyo/Paris
Project team: Jean De Gastines, Daisuke Sugawara, Marc Ferrand
Project management: Stefano Tagliacarne
Project team, Institute of Design/ Lahti Polytechnic: Vesa Ijäs, Jari Kantola (Professors), Petra Eronen, Elina Helminen, Harri Homi, Esa Hyytiäinen, Sami Lyytikäinen, Katja Rauhamäki, Aino Vaulasvirta, Hanna Östman
Structural engineer: Terrell International; Zbigniew Koszut; CeAS, Giovanni Canetta
Electrical engineer: Milano Progetti, Arturo Busà, Enrico Schiatti
General contractor: Falt Design, Francesco Tibaldi
Completion: 2007

www.shigerubanarchitects.com
tokyo@shigerubanarchitects.com
europe@shigerubanarchitects.com

Shigeru Ban
see left

Audi Center in Munich

Client: Mahag Unternehmens-
gruppe, Munich
Architects: Allmann Sattler
Wappner Architekten, Munich
Project manager: Karin Hengher
Project team: Michael Frank,
Kai Homm
Structural engineer: Werner Sobek
Ingenieure, Stuttgart
Electrical engineer:
Raible + Partner, Munich
Landscape architect: Realgrün
Landschaftsarchitekten, Munich
General contractor: Xaver Riebel
Holding GmbH & Co. KG,
Mindelheim
Completion: 2008

www.allmannsattlerwappner.de
info@allmannsattlerwappner.de

Markus Allmann
Born 1959, Ludwigshafen; 1986
Diploma, TU Munich; 2005–2006
guest professor, Peter Behrens
School of Architecture, Düsseldorf;
2006–present Professor, University
of Stuttgart

Amandus Sattler
Born 1957 in Marktredwitz; 1985
Diploma, TU Munich; 2005–present:
teaching position, Academy of
Fine Arts Munich; 2007 teaching
position, École Nationale Supérieur
d'Architecture de Nancy, France;
2009 guest professor, FH Cologne

Ludwig Wappner
Born 1957 in Hösbach; 1985
Diploma, TU Munich; guest
professor, Stuttgart University of
Applied Sciences

1987 founding of Architekturbüro
Allmann Sattler, Munich; 1993
expansion, Allmann Sattler
Wappner Architekten

adidas Brand Center in Herzogenaurach

Client: adidas AG,
Herzogenaurach
Architects: querkraft Architekten,
Vienna
Project manager: Erwin Stättner
Project team: Carmen Hottinger,
Sandra Schiel, Dominique Dinies,
Bernward Krone
Construction management:
Haushoch Architekten, Nuremberg
Structural engineer:
werkraum, Vienna
Mechanical/electrical engineer:
Ingenieurbüro Gerhard Duschl,
Rosenheim
Landscape architect:
Adler & Olesch, Nuremberg
Fire prevention: Ingenieurbüro
Stümpert-Strunk, Ludwigshafen
Building physics: Ingenieurbüro
Walter Prause, Vienna
Completion: 2006

www.querkraft.at
office@querkraft.at

Gerd Erhartt
Born 1964 in Vienna; 1992 Diploma,
TU Vienna; 1994–1998 Büro Dunkl,
Erhartt; 2001–2004 teaching
position, TU Vienna

Peter Sapp
Born 1961 in Linz; 1994 Diploma,
TU Vienna; 2006–present Professor
for Interior Design, Academy of
Fine Arts Munich

Jakob Dunkl
Born in 1963 in Frankfurt am Main;
1990 Diploma, TU Vienna;
1994–1998 Büro Dunkl, Erhartt;
2001–2004 guest professor, Roger
Williams University, Bristol USA

1998 founding of querkraft
Architekten (with Michael Zinner
1998–2004)

Baufritz exhibition building in Erkheim

Client: Firma Baufritz, Erkheim
Architects: a.ml und partner,
Nuremberg; Matthias Loebermann
Project team: Berit Richter
Structural engineer: Ingenieurbüro
Ulm, Uttenreuth
Lighting planning: Michael Schmidt,
Munich
Landscape architect:
Christine Volm, Sindelfingen
Building art: Agnes Keil,
Memmingen
Completion: 2005

www.aml-partner.de
mail@aml-partner.de

Matthias Loebermann
Born 1964 in Nuremberg;
1984–1990 architecture studies,
University of Stuttgart; 1984–1988
art painting studies, Stuttgart
State Academy of Art and Design;
1996 founding of architectural
office a.ml und partner, Nuremberg; 2002 Professor, FH Biberach

"Freudenhaus" optician store in Munich

Client: Freudenhaus Optik
Handels GmbH, Munich
Architects: AIGNER ARCHITEC-
TURE, Munich
Project manager: Marie Aigner
Construction management:
Marcus Beuerlein, Marie Aigner
General contractor, interior:
Bauer innovativ GmbH, Altötting
Completion: 2008

www.aigner-architecture.com
info@aigner-architecture.com

Marie Aigner
Born 1972 in Mallersdorf; Architec-
ture studies, TU Munich and Ecole
d'Architecture de Paris-la-Seine;
collaboration for Richard Meier,
New York and SOM Architects
Skidmore Owings Merrill, New
York; 2003 founding of AIGNER
ARCHITECTURE, Munich

Whiteleys Shopping Center in London

Client: Ford McDonald/Food Inc., London
Architects: Lifschutz Davidson Sandilands, London
Project team: Silvano Cranchi, Cordula Stach, Ellen Schäfer, Robert de Boni
Kitchen planner: Exclusive Ranges Ltd., Welwyn Garden City
Lighting planning: Equation Lighting Design, London
Project coordination: Davis Langdon, London
Structural engineer: Fluid Structurer
Completion: 2008

www.lds-uk.com
mail@lds-uk.com

Paul Sandilands
1976 apprenticeship, engineering; 1980–87 studies, Birmingham Polytechnic and Manchester University; architect in Birmingham; 1988–1992 collaborator for Lifschutz Davidson; 1992–present partner, Lifschutz Davidson Sandilands

MPREIS Supermarket in Innsbruck

Client: MPREIS Warenvertriebs GmbH, Völs
Architects: Rainer Köberl, Innsbruck
Project team: Michael Steinlechner
Project manager: Klaus Schmücking, Inzing
Structural engineer: Alfred Brunnsteiner, Natters
Mechanical engineer: Tivoli Plan, Gerhard Lippautz, Innsbruck
Electrical engineer: HG-engineering, Thomas Haslinger, Innsbruck
Lighting planning: Rainer Köberl and Halotech, Innsbruck
Completion: 2004

www.rainerkoeberl.at
rainer.koeberl@aon.at
atelier.koeberl@aon.at

Rainer Köberl
Born 1956 in Innsbruck; 1976–1984 studies, Innsbruck and Haifa, Israel; 1992 founding of architecture office in Innsbruck; 1993–1999 teaching position, Institute for Urban Planning and Design, Building Science and Design, Technical Faculty, University of Innsbruck; 1998–2002 co-founder and lecturer, Academy of Design Bolzano

Edeka Supermarket in Ingolstadt

Client: EDEKA Handelsgesellschaft Südbayern mbH, Ingolstadt; ALUEDA-Markt Ingolstadt GmbH, Gaimersheim
Corporate Architecture Concept: Christoph M. Achammer, Robert Kelca, Marc Eutebach, Andreas Fricke, Rudolf Pfister, Martin Lukasser
Architects: ATP Architekten und Ingenieure, Munich
Project managers: Andreas Herrscher, Martin Lukasser
Structural engineer: bwp Burggraf, Weichinger+Partner GmbH, Munich
Mechanical engineer: ATP Architekten und Ingenieure, Munich
Landscape architect: Stefanie Jühling, Munich
Completion: 2006

www.atp.ag
info@atp.ag

Christoph M. Achammer
Born 1957 in Innsbruck; architecture studies, TU Vienna; 1987–present partner, ATP Architekten und Ingenieure, Munich; 2001–present Professor, Chair for Industrial Construction and Interdisciplinary Construction Planning, TU Vienna

Noise barrier with integrated car showroom near Utrecht

Client: Hessing Holding BV, Utrecht (car showroom); Projectbureau Leidsche Rijn, Utrecht (noise barrier)
Architects: ONL [Oosterhuis_ Lénárd] BV, Rotterdam; Kas Oosterhuis, Ilona Lénárd
Project manager: Sander Boer (car showroom), Cas Aalbers (noise barrier)
Project team: Gijs Joosen, Gerard van den Engel, Tom Hals, Dimitar Karanikolov, Ines Moreira, Vladin Petrov, Tom Smith, Richard Lewis, Andrei Badescu, Maciek Swiatkowsky, Barbara Janssen, Rafael Seemann, Bas de Beer, Ronald Brandsma
Construction management: Meijers Staalbouw BV, Serooskerke
Structural engineer: Van der Vorm Engineering, Maarssen (car showroom), Faktor BV, Middelburg (noise barrier)
Mechanical/electrical engineer: Installatiebedrijf Andriessen, Houten
Completion: 2005

www.oosterhuis.nl
info@oosterhuis.nl

Kas Oosterhuis
Born 1951 in Amersfoort; studies, TU Delft; 1989 founding of Kas Oosterhuis Architekten; 2000–present Professor, research group TU Delft

Ilona Lénárd
Born in Hungary; 1971 Theater Academy Budapest; 1983 Willem de Kooning Academy for Visual Art, Rotterdam

2004 founding of architecture office ONL [Oosterhuis_ Lénárd] BV, Rotterdam

Exhibition hall in Paris

Client: Sipac, Paris
Architects: Anne Lacaton & Jean
Philippe Vassal, Paris
Project team: Marion Cadran,
Emmanuelle Delage, Benjamin
Dubreu, Frédéric Hérard
Construction management:
Sipac, Paris
Structural engineer: Cesma, Bor-
deaux; Batiserf Ingenierie, Fontaine
Mechanical engineer:
SNC Lavallin, Créteil
Electrical engineer: T3E, Alfortville
Landscape architect:
Cyrille Marlin, Pau
Fire prevention:
Vulcaneo, Courbevoie
Completion: 2007

www.lacatonvassal.com
lacaton.vassal@wanadoo.fr
mail@lacatonvassal.com

Anne Lacaton
Born 1955 in Saint Pardoux, France;
1980 Diploma, Ecole d'Architecture
de Bordeaux; 1984 Diploma, Urban
Planning, University of Bordeaux;
2003–2004 guest professor, Technical University Lausanne (EPFL)

Jean Philippe Vassal
Born 1954 in Casablanca, Marocco;
1980 Diploma, Ecole d'Architecture
de Bordeaux; 1992–2005 guest
professor in Bordeaux, Versailles,
Düsseldorf; 2007–present guest
professor, TU Berlin

1987 founding of architectural office
Anne Lacaton & Jean Philippe
Vassal, Bordeaux; later Paris

New Trade Fair in Stuttgart

Client: Projektgesellschaft
Neue Messe GmbH & Co. KG,
Stuttgart; Flughafen Stuttgart GmbH
(parking garage)
Architects: Wulf & Partner, Stuttgart;
Tobias Wulf, Kai Bierich, Alexander
Vohl
Landscape architect:
Adler + Olesch, Nuremberg
Structural engineer: Mayr +
Ludescher Beratende Ingenieure
GmbH, Stuttgart (halls); Leonhardt,
Andrä und Partner Beratende
Ingenieure VBI GmbH, Stuttgart
(parking garage); Boll und Partner
Beratende Ingenieure VBI, Stuttgart
(congress center)
Mechanical engineer: Brandi IGH
Ingenieure GmbH, Ostfildern;
Scholze Ingenieurgesellschaft
mbH, Leinfelden-Echterdingen
Electrical engineer: ibb Burrer &
Deuring Ingenieurbüro GmbH,
Ludwigsburg
Facade designer: Erich Mosbacher
Planungsbüro für Fassadentechnik,
Friedrichshafen
Lighting planning:
Bartenbach LichtLabor GmbH,
Aldrans/Innsbruck
Signage and guidance systems:
Büro Uebele Visuelle Kommunika-
tion, Stuttgart
Completion: 2007

www.wulf-partner.de
info@wulf-partner.de

1987 founding of office Tobias Wulf
1996 founding of Architekturbüro
Wulf & Partner, Stuttgart by Tobias
Wulf, Kai Bierich and Alexander Vohl.

Stylepark Lounge in Berlin

Client: Stylepark, Frankfurt am Main
Architects: J. MAYER H., Berlin;
Jürgen Mayer H.
Project team: Sebastian Finckh
Project partners: Sikkens,
Gira, Dornbracht, Garpa
Completion: 2001

www.jmayerh.de
contact@jmayerh.de

Jürgen Mayer H.
Born 1965 in Stuttgart; architecture
studies, University of Stuttgart,
The Cooper Union New York,
Princeton University; 1996 founding
of J. MAYER H. Architects, Berlin;
1996–present teaching positions,
Berlin University of the Arts,
Harvard University Graduate Scool
of Design, Architectual Association
London, Columbia University New
York, University of Toronto Canada

Exhibition stand "Garment Garden" in Frankfurt am Main

Client: Nya Nordiska, Dannenberg
Architects: J. MAYER H., Berlin;
Jürgen Mayer H.
Project team: Alessandra Raponi,
Simon Takasaki
Completion: 2006

www.jmayerh.de
contact@jmayerh.de

Jürgen Mayer H.
see left

Eternit exhibition stands in Stuttgart and Munich

Client: Eternit AG, Heidelberg
Architects: Astrid Bornheim
Architektur, Berlin
Project team: Alexander Butz,
Jan Pingel, Nico Schwarzer
Exhibition construction: Zeissig
GmbH & Co. KG, Springe
Completion: 2008 + 2009

www.astridbornheim.de
info@astridbornheim.de

Astrid Bornheim
Born 1969 in Bad Honnef; 1998
Diploma, TU Braunschweig;
1999-present Assistant Professor,
Institute for Construction Design
TU Braunschweig; 2003 founding of
architectural office Astrid Bornheim
Architektur, Berlin; 2004–2005
teaching position, Urban Labora-
tory New York, Institute of
Technology in Berlin; 2004–2008
teaching position, University of
Nottingham, London.

E.ON exhibition stand in Essen

Client: E.ON Energy Sales GmbH,
Munich
Architects: avcommunication
GmbH, Ludwigsburg/Munich
Project team: Adrian von Starck,
Andreas Olbrich, Ulrike Hommel,
Stefan Meyer, Markus Mögel,
Sandra Kessler
Project manager:
Nikola B. Wischnewsky
Exhibition construction: mac
messe- und ausstellungscenter
Service GmbH, Langenlonsheim
Media technology: Gahrens +
Battermann GmbH, Korntal
Completion: 2008

www.avcommunication.com
av@avcommunication.com

avcommunication GmbH, founded
in 1982 by Norbert W. Daldrop in
Stuttgart, is an independent agency
for communication and design.
Core competencies feature design,
conceptualization and creation of
comprehensive brand dramatizations for trade shows, events,
incentives, and exhibitions. The
portfolio of services is complemented by the independent
subsidiary for film and interactive
media productions, publishing, and
traditional advertisement. Offices
are located in Ludwigsburg,
Munich, Hamburg, and Berlin.

Serafini exhibition stand in Cologne

Client: Paul Serafini GmbH & Co.
KG, Iserlohn
Architects: atelier 522, Markdorf
Exhibition construction:
Standhaft Messebau, Neuss
Completion: 2009

www.atelier522.com
atelier@atelier522.com

The creative office atelier 522 was
founded in 2006 by Philipp Beck
and is active in architecture, interior
architecture, product design,
graphics, and photography.

Authors

Christian Schittich (Ed.)
Born 1956;
architecture studies, TU Munich;
7 years professional experience in architecture, publishing activity;
1991–present editorial team DETAIL International Journal for Architecture and Construction Details;
1992–1998 managing editor, 1998–present editor-in-chief;
author and editor of numerous architectural books and publications.

Ruedi Baur
Born 1956;
studies, graphic design, School of Applied Arts, Zurich;
1983 co-founder, Atelier BBV, Lyon, Milan, Zurich;
1989 founding of Atelier intégral ruedi baur, Paris, Zurich (2002), Berlin (2007)
1999 founding, Institute for Interdisciplinary Design 2id, Leipzig;
April 2004–present director and founder of Design2context Research Institute at the Zurich University of the Arts (ZHdK);
2007 founding of Laboratoire IRB, Paris;
2007–present teaching position, ENSAD, Paris;
author of numerous publications.

Heike Gfrereis
Born 1968;
studies, German Language and Literature Studies, Art History, University of Stuttgart; scientific collaborator, University of Stuttgart;
collaboration for Atelier Knut Lohrer, Stuttgart, responsible for conceptualization, dramaturgy, and audiovisual media;
2001–present director, Schiller National Museum (German Literature Archive, Marbach), 2006 inclusion of Museum of Modern Literature, curator of permanent exhibitions and various temporary exhibitions;
author of numerous publications on literature theory and exhibition theory.

Claudia Luxbacher
Born 1974;
studies, Art History, University of Nürnberg-Erlangen, Vienna, Padua;
internship, Palatinate Gallery of Art, Kaiserslautern;
2006–present director for press and public relations, ATELIER BRÜCKNER;
freelance curator and journalist.

Eberhard Schlag
Born 1967;
architectural studies, University of Stuttgart, Illinois Institute of Technology Chicago;
architectural collaboration in offices in Stuttgart and Berlin;
1997–present collaboration for ATELIER BRÜCKNER; partner and executive member;
lecturer at various Universities.

HG Merz
Born 1947;
architecture studies, University of Stuttgart;
professional activity, architect, curator, exhibition designer with offices in Stuttgart and Berlin;
teaching position, experimental design, TU Darmstadt;
focus on conceptualization, development, and implementation of museums and exhibition designs as well as historic preservation.

Patrick Wais
Born 1975;
studies, Philosophy and Sociology, University of Tübingen;
2007–present scientific collaborator, hg merz architekten museumsgestalter, Stuttgart;
focus on conceptualization and content-based development of exhibitions in architecture, aesthetics, and object culture.

Jons Messedat
Born 1965;
architecture studies, University of Stuttgart, industrial design, Stuttgart State Academy of Art and Design;
1994 architect, Foster + Partners, London, Berlin;
1998 scientific collaborator, Bauhaus University Weimar, doctorate thesis on Corporate Architecture;
2004–present director, Institute for Corporate Architecture, Stuttgart;
teaching position, University of Applied Sciences Cologne, Corporate Architecture master course, University of Applied Sciences Nordwestschweiz, Zollverein School Essen;
jury member for international architectural and design competitions.

Thomas Schielke
Born 1973;
architecture studies, TU Darmstadt;
2001–present responsible for didactic communication for lighting manufacturer ERCO;
teaching position for architectural lighting at various Universities.

Susanne Schmidhuber
Born 1956;
interior architecture studies, Rosenheim University of Applied Sciences;
collaboration for Architekturbüro Denk Mauder & Partner, Munich;
1984 founding of Schmidhuber + Partner with Klaus Schmidhuber;
manager, Schmidhuber + Partner, Munich;
membership, ADC (Art Director's Club Germany).

Günther Röckl
Born 1943;
studies, exhibition design, Art Academy Berlin, Swiss Marketing and Advertising Institute, Dübendorf;
1992–1999 manager, MERO Switzerland GmbH;
1999–present manager, MERO Exhibit Systems Distribution Switzerland, Austria, Bavaria;
lecturer, trade show marketing, Swiss Marketing and Advertising Institute;
membership, EXPO & EVENT SWISS ASSOCIATION;
author (event and trade show marketing).

Illustration credits

The authors and editor wish to extend their sincere thanks to all those who helped to realize this book by making illustrations available. All drawings contained in this volume have been specially prepared in-house. Photos without credits are form the architects' own archives or the archives of "DETAIL, Review of Architecture". Despite intense efforts, it was not possible to identify the copyright owners of certain photos and illustrations. Their rights remain unaffected, however, and we request them to contact us.

from photographers, photo archives and image agencies:
· pp. 8, 72, 73 bottom, 74, 75, 76/77:
Schaefer, A. T., Stuttgart
· p. 10 top:
Denancé, Michel, Paris
· p. 10 bottom:
Binet, Hélène, London
· pp. 11 top, 130–132:
Ruault, Philippe, Nantes
· pp. 11 bottom, 14 bottom, 43 bottom, 44 top, 48, 50 top, middle, 91 top, 93, 166 middle, bottom:
Schittich, Christian, Munich
· p. 12:
akg-images, Berlin
· p. 15 top:
Alagheband, Fariborz, Doha, Qatar
· p. 15 bottom:
McIntosh, Jonathan, Boston
· pp. 16 top, 17 middle, 20 bottom, 21:
Bundesarchiv, Koblenz
· p. 16 bottom:
Library of Congress, Prints and Photographs Collection, Washington
· p. 17 top:
Kneidl, Dietmar, Schönau
· p. 17 bottom:
Troitskaya, Irina, Moscow
· p. 18 top:
Kecko, Rheineck, Switzerland
· p. 18 bottom:
Sandstein/wikimedia.org
· p. 20 top:
The Brooklyn Museum, Goodyear Archival Collection, New York
· pp. 22 bottom, 25:
Huthmacher, Werner/artur, Essen
· pp. 23, 52, 53, 56:
Halbe, Roland, Stuttgart
· p. 24 top, middle:
Bryant, Richard/arcaid, Kingston-upon-Thames

· p. 24 bottom:
Huthmacher, Werner, Berlin
· pp. 26, 27:
Ansel Associates Inc., Point Richmond
· p. 29:
Baan, Iwan, Amsterdam
· pp. 30, 35, 57 left, 59 top:
Willock, Nathan/View/artur, Essen
· pp. 31, 32:
Richters, Christian, Münster
· p. 33:
Malagamba, Duccio, Barcelona
· p. 34 left:
Deutsches Literaturarchiv Marbach
· p. 34 right:
Müller-Naumann, Stefan/artur, Essen
· pp. 37–41:
Heinrich, Michael, Munich
· pp. 42, 45 bottom, 50 bottom
Buck, Markus, Munich
· pp. 44 bottom, 45 top, 46, 49, 51:
Holzherr, Florian, Munich
· p. 54:
González, Brigida/UNStudio
· pp. 57 right, 58, 59 bottom, 60, 64 middle, bottom, 65, 68 middle, bottom, 69:
González, Brigida, Stuttgart
· p. 66:
Meinel, Udo, Berlin
· pp. 70, 71:
Haus der Geschichte / Bernd Eidenmüller, Stuttgart
· pp. 81–83:
Boy de la Tour, Didier, Paris
· pp. 84, 85:
Schweigert, Sabine, Milan
· pp. 86, 90 bottom:
Zumtobel, Dornbirn
· p. 87:
Janssen, Carsten, Alfeld an der Leine
· p. 88:
Associazione Archivio Storico Olivetti, Ivrea, Italy
· p. 89:
Triad, Berlin
· p. 90 top:
Kaldewei, Ahlen
· p. 91 bottom:
Tännler, Roland, Zurich
· pp. 92 top, 118–121:
Schaller, Lukas, Vienna
· p. 92 bottom:
Wett, G. R., Innsbruck
· p. 94 top:
Branded Bricks GmbH, Berlin
· p. 94 bottom:
Pulat, Murat, Istanbul
· p. 95:
Mair, Walter, Zurich
· pp. 96, 97, 99 right:
Passoth, Jens, Berlin

· pp. 100–103:
Hagen, Gerhard/artur, Essen
· pp. 104–107:
Hacke, Mila, Berlin
· pp. 108, 109 top left, bottom, 110, 111:
ERCO, Lüdenscheid
· pp. 112–114:
Pipo, Florian, Munich
· pp. 115–117:
Hill, Alex, Brighton
· pp. 122–125:
Engelhardt/Sellin Architekturfotografie, Aschau
· pp. 126–129:
Hoekstra, Rob, Kalmhout
· pp. 134, 136, 139, 162 middle, bottom, 163–165:
Halbe, Roland/artur, Essen
· p. 135:
Vogt, Steffen/Archigraphie, Stuttgart
· pp. 140, 146, 147:
Keller, Andreas, Altdorf
· pp. 143, 144 bottom:
Müller-Naumann, Stefan, Munich
· p. 144 top:
Studio Schroll, Hagen
· p. 145 top, middle:
Vohler, Christoph, Munich
· p. 148:
Oberle, Wolfgang, Munich
· p. 149 top:
Katzer, Simon, Munich
· p. 149 bottom:
Struve, Nina, Hamburg
· pp. 150 right, 151:
Walter, Uwe, Berlin
· pp. 152, 153 bottom:
Constantin Meyer Photographie, Cologne
· p. 155:
MERO-TSK International GmbH & Co. KG, Würzburg
· pp. 156–161:
Franck, David, Ostfildern
· p. 167:
P2 Photo Production, Düsseldorf
· p. 168 bottom 1st column:
Double, Steve, London
· p. 168 bottom 2nd column:
Okamoto, Takashi, Tokyo
· p. 168 bottom 3rd column:
Knight, Nick, London
· p. 169 bottom 3rd column:
Koopmann, Miranda, Utrecht
· p. 171 bottom 1st column:
Wesener, Wolfgang
· p. 173 bottom 3rd column:
Helbig, Oliver, Berlin

from books and journals:
· p. 14 top:
Burns, Stanley, A Morning's Work – Medical Photographs from the

Burns Archive and Collection 1843–1939, Santa Fe, 1998
· p. 14 middle:
Bayer, Herbert, Visual Communication Architecture Painting, New York, 1967
· p. 18 middle:
Das Wissen des 20. Jahrhunderts, Rheda, 1931

Articles and introductory b/w photos:
· p. 8:
"That's Opera" traveling exhibition, ATELIER BRÜCKNER, Stuttgart
· p. 12:
Crystal Palace, London, Joseph Paxton
· p. 60:
Glass collection, State Museum of Württemberg, Stuttgart, hg merz architekten museumsgestalter, Stuttgart
· p. 86:
Zumtobel Light Forum, Dornbirn, Herbert Resch, Aysil Sari, Dornbirn
· p. 140:
Audi exhibition stand, IAA 2007 Frankfurt, Schmidhuber + Partner, Munich

Dust-jacket:
BMW Museum in Munich
Architects:
ATELIER BRÜCKNER, Stuttgart
Photo:
Christian Schittich, Munich

Project data are provided as is by the responsible architectural offices. The publisher is not responsible for correctness of provided data.